THE WORLD WILDLIFE FUND BOOK OF
ORCHIDS

THE WORLD WILDLIFE FUND BOOK OF
ORCHIDS

By Jack Kramer

Foreword by Mark J. Plotkin,
Plant Conservation Director, the World Wildlife Fund

Abbeville Press · Publishers · New York

Editor: Susan Costello
Designer: Molly Shields
Production manager: Dana Cole

Jacket photograph, front: *Cattleya* Landate. Hermann Pigors
Jacket photograph, back: Potinara 'Edwin Hausermann'. Hermann Pigors
page 1: *Phalaenopsis* Class President 'Willowbrook'. Hermann Pigors.
page 2: Slc. Jewel Box 'Dark Waters'. Hermann Pigors.
pages 4–5: Rntda. Seminole. Charles Marden Fitch.
page 6: *Dendrobium Victoriae reginae* 'Veronica'. Charles Marden Fitch.

Library of Congress Cataloging-in-Publication Data
Kramer, Jack, 1927–
   The World Wildlife Fund book of orchids.

   Bibliography: p.
   Includes index.
   1. Orchids.   2. Orchid culture.   I. World Wildlife Fund.   II. Title.
SB409.K73   1989   635.9′3415   89-6591
ISBN 1-55859-001-3

The first edition, *Orchids: Flowers of Romance and Mystery*, was published in 1975 by
Harry N. Abrams, Inc.

Author's Note:

Many of the orchids photographed for this book were from my own collection gathered
over a period of fifteen years in Chicago, Illinois, and Marin County, California. The
plants were grown in a garden room in average home conditions, and my former shop
(The Garden District) in the Napa Valley.

CONTENTS

Preface

The past ten years have been witness to incredible strides in the hybridization of orchids, leading to mammoth leaps in the popularity of these treasured plants. When it was decided that my book *Orchids: Flowers of Mystery and Romance*, which was published in 1975, was to be updated and revised, we decided to include new introductions, a chapter on cultivating orchids, and information on improvements in the world of orchids. While the first edition concentrated on species, this expanded version includes many hybrids—those crossbred plants that have been developed in recent years, such as Odontiodas, Ascocendas, and many new Cattleyas (the most popular group of orchids).

The original orchid history and legends remain, but the rest of the text has been updated and most of the black and white photographs have been replaced with magnificent color portraits. Many new plants have been added to bring you the most impressive gallery of glorious orchids ever photographed and presented in one volume.

The original book, begun almost two decades ago, is now a collector's item. The new and expanded volume is now offered for all orchid lovers—beginners, hobbyists, and nongardeners alike.

10   Orchids

Foreword

On more than one occasion, while traveling through the Amazon on ethnobotanical expeditions, I have looked up to see extraordinary orchids growing on the bark of forest trees. I have always felt that I was looking at one of the great works of art—but it was art created not by the hand of man, but by the genius of mother nature.

The botanical conservationist faces a daunting task: to interest the general public in the conservation of plants. Until relatively recently, most people concerned with international conservation issues were intrigued by what have been called the "charismatic mega-vertebrates"—elephants, rhinos, pandas and the like. In contrast, plant species can hardly compete with the emotional appeal of the endangered wildlife. Orchids, however, are an exception; they are a godsend to the plant conservationist.

Invariably the plants most people associate with the tropics are palms and orchids. Palms *are* the roots of life in the tropics, providing local people with all the basic necessities (food, shelter, fuel, and fiber) as well as many of the ameliorants (spices, oils, waxes, gums, poisons, and medicines). Yet despite their extraordinary utility, palms lack the aesthetic appeal of the orchid family. There is something ethereal and sublime about the flowers of many orchids, one of the most populous families on earth.

Scientists currently estimate that there are approximately thirty-five thousand species of orchids in the world, but they are not evenly distributed. Although several species have been discovered within the Arctic Circle, most species are found in the tropics. Colombia alone may be home to thirty-five hundred species—10 percent of the world's orchid flora. The island of Madagascar, off the coast of Mozambique, comprises only 2 percent of the land mass of continental Africa, yet it has more species of orchids than are found in all the countries of Africa combined. Expeditions to tropical regions around the world continue to find new species.

Orchids are fascinating to biologists not only because of their beauty but because of the incredible diversity found within the orchid family. Species may range in height from less than one inch (2.5 centimeters) to over ten feet (thirty meters). Most orchids are herbaceous, but some resemble vines while others look like shrubs. Orchids may be terrestrial, epiphytic, lithophytic, semiaquatic or, in the case of several Australian forms, subterranean. In fact, one species seems almost marine—while traveling in the Choco region of western Colombia, I found a little *Brassavola* growing above the waterline on boulders in the Pacific!

The fabulous *Dendrobium nobile* has always been a prized orchid; today there are many wonderful varieties. The masses of flowers, illustrated here, are not the imagination of the artist, since these dendrobiums do produce a profusion of blossoms.

Because of their astounding variety, orchids have attracted the attention of many major scientific figures. Linneaus was fascinated by them and Charles Darwin wrote a book on orchids. Darwin was particularly intrigued by the extraordinary coevolution between these plants and their animal pollinators. After studying a Madagascan orchid of the genus *Angraecum* which featured nectar hidden at the bottom of a long ovary, Darwin predicted that a moth with a ten-inch (twenty–five centimeter) proboscis would be found in Madagascar. Although his contemporaries scoffed at his prediction, a moth fitting this description was subsequently collected.

The ancient Greek physician Dioscorides used orchids to treat sexual problems. The name "orchid" is derived from the Greek word for "testicle" and describes the testicular-shaped tubers found on many European species. Dioscorides and his followers were believers in the so-called Doctrine of Signatures, which stemmed from the belief that God had created plants for man's use and enjoyment and had placed a sign on each species to indicate its utilitarian value. The herbals and medical books of Europe during the Middle Ages are replete with references to the medicinal properties of orchids.

Today, however, orchids do not serve as sources of important medications. Although alkaloids were found in species of *Dendrobium* as early as 1892, most phytochemists have long considered the orchid family to be relatively inert from a chemical standpoint. Recent investigation at the Botanical Museum of Harvard University indicates that orchids are much more alkaloid-rich than was previously supposed; in fact, over 30 percent of the species analyzed were found to contain alkaloids, many of which are the type that may prove useful for modern medicine.

From an economic standpoint, the most important orchid is vanilla (*Vanilla planifolia*), yet it is near extinction in some areas. Although native to tropical America, most of the commercial production now takes place in Madagascar, Reunion and the Comoros. Since the insects which pollinate the plant in its native habitat are not found on these islands, the vanilla plants must be pollinated by hand. Demand for vanilla continues to increase, and the forests of Madagascar are being cut down to expand the vanilla plantations. At the same time, the forests of Mexico where vanilla is native are also being destroyed for peasant agriculture, thus narrowing the natural gene pool which, if crossed with cultivated vanilla, might increase the yield and resistance to pests and diseases.

Yet the vanilla plants of Mexico are not the only orchids facing extinction. The twin evils of habitat destruction and over-collection for the horticultural trade threaten orchids around the world. For example, at least one of the forty-nine species native to Great Britain is believed to be extinct. The national flower of Colombia, *Cattleya trianae*, is already rare in the wild. In Venezuela, the famous "Island of Orchids" (*Isla de las Orquideas*) in Canaima National Park has been all but stripped of its orchids by over-zealous collectors. What is to be done?

In 1984, following the 11th World Orchid Congress, the International Union for the Conservation of Nature (IUCN) authorized the establishment of an Orchid Specialist Group to coordinate conservation activities focusing on orchids. Since the establishment of this group, leading conservation organizations like World Wildlife Fund and the Center for Plant Conservation have joined forces with major institutions like the Missouri Botanical Garden and the Arnold Arboretum to preserve and protect orchids for future generations. At WWF, we are:

—supporting Mexican colleagues who are working to establish the conservation status of *Phragmipedium exstaminodium*. This extraordinarily showy species is known only from two small populations, one probably extinct and the other severely threatened;

—working with Venezuelan colleagues to develop a database for determining conservation priorities for local orchids; and

—collaborating with Colombian colleagues to develop a network of protected areas deemed critical for the survival of endemic orchids.

Given the increasing rates of habitat destruction and collection of orchids for the horticultural trade, the fight to save the orchids is just getting underway. We need to alert the general public to the challenge we are facing. I cannot think of any evidence more convincing of the ethereal beauty of the orchid family than this extraordinary book from Abbeville Press. Many books on orchids have already been published yet none surpass the beauty of this volume. The quality of these photographs will do more for orchid conservation than all of the scientific monographs on the Orchidaceae ever published.

Mark J. Plotkin, Ph.D.
World Wildlife Fund
Washington, D.C.

Introduction

The first orchid I ever saw was the corsage my mother was given on special occasions, generally once a year on her birthday. It was a gaudy bright lavender flower of the genus *Cattleya*, perfected by man to excel in size and color.

While most of us think of the cattleya as *the* orchid, few people realize that some thirty thousand species of orchids grow wild all over the world—from Alaska to the antipodes. Recently, many of these have become houseplants, and today orchids are, like African violets, indoor favorites.

The wonderful world of flowers is almost limitless, and members of the family Orchidaceae are outstanding for their drama, color, and form. It has taken us over one hundred years to explode the myth that orchids could not survive unless they were sealed under glass like rare gems in treasure houses. Today, we know that orchids can be grown as easily as any other plant— perhaps even more easily because many of them have water-storage vessels (pseudobulbs) to keep them alive if we sometimes forget to tend them (presupposing that they receive adequate light and the proper growing temperature).

Now that orchids have become popular indoor plants, it is useful to learn something about them—where they come from, how they grow in nature, why some grow on mountainsides, others on trees or on the ground. It is time to find out what has made them so appealing and desirable through the years, and to investigate the myths and superstitions that have led to the mystique of the orchid.

In spite of their beauty and desirability, orchids are perhaps the most misunderstood of flowers. But when we separate fact from fancy, we discover their true and fascinating stories. First, let us eliminate a few of the more popular fantasies. Orchids are not carnivorous or parasitic; they have no malefic methods of propagation, no secret devices to enhance their beauty. Orchids are merely the result of nature performing at her best—creating the dazzling array of colors, shapes, and textures that make these flowers among the most beautiful known.

While there are a number of books on how to grow orchids, there are few volumes on the plants themselves. Here I shall concentrate on the plant and its background, but I will also describe growing methods that I have found to be successful. Included are the best possible photographs, mostly in color, which show the true beauty of the plants as they really are—the exquisite texture, the incredible form, the dramatic character of the flower. I only wish that photographs could convey scent, because some orchids have such a lovely fragrance.

Many of the orchids in this book are from my collection and were photographed in my garden room. Mainly, they are species orchids, free from the hand of man, but many new hybrid orchids derived from cattleyas and cymbidiums, which most people recognize on sight, are also included.

It was difficult to make a selection from the many thousands I have grown over the years. The final decision was based not so much on the availability of the orchid but on its beauty. Some are rare, many are common; some simply did not photograph well, others did. In all, hundreds of plants were photographed over the years. The best of the collection is shown in this book. If your favorite orchid is missing, it is not by deliberate act but because of limitations of space or time.

Botanical names of orchids are changed occasionally as taxonomists continue their research, and plants that have been classified for years in one genus are sometimes relegated to another. No doubt there will be further changes in botanical nomenclature by the time this book goes to press.

The genus *Cypripedium* (lady's-slipper orchids) for years included *Paphiopedilum*, *Phragmipedium*, and sometimes *Selenipedium*. Today, many authorities consider these as entirely different genera. They are so treated in this book.

In this volume I have tried to arrange the plants shown in their genera as they are accepted by most growers and as they are listed in suppliers' catalogues. I have used the scientific and common names widely accepted, without trying to define the borderline species that still puzzle taxonomists. The names of hybrids and cultivars are sometimes redefined; with the tremendous amount of orchid hybridization being done it is almost impossible to be up-to-the-minute about names. So you may find an orchid here not officially registered or a variety not universally accepted under a specific name.

Through the years I have grown hundreds of orchids and written several books on how to grow them. As I discovered the secrets of caring for the plants, I began to wonder why they so captivated and intrigued me—and countless others. (Even nongardeners have a fondness for orchids.) What is the lure of orchids? Their history reveals stories of adventure as exciting as the flowers themselves. Knowing their stories has given me a greater appreciation of the plants, and I hope, through this book, to enhance your enjoyment of the Orchidaceae.

Jack Kramer
Napa, California

16 Orchids

History

The Greeks to Linnaeus

In antiquity and during the Middle Ages, orchids, like many other plants, were used chiefly for their supposed medicinal properties, especially as aphrodisiacs. Mediterranean orchids were small, temperate-zone species, barely resembling the large and colorful corsage flowers we know today.

The word *orchis*, from which the whole family received its name, was first used for this purpose by the Greek philosopher Theophrastus (c. 372–c. 287 B.C.), a pupil of Aristotle. Theophrastus is sometimes called the father of botany. In his manuscript *Enquiry into Plants*, *orchis* (meaning testis) referred to the underground tuberous roots of the Mediterranean orchis, which are similar in shape to testicles.

For the next three hundred years orchids remained unnoted in the plant world, but they were mentioned again in the first century A.D. by Dioscorides, a Greek physician in Asia Minor, who collected information on medicinal plants while serving as surgeon in Nero's Roman army. In his chief work, *Materia medica*, he describes some five hundred plants, designating two of them *orchis*, from Theophrastus' work. Because the orchis tubers resembled testicles, he hypothesized that the plants influenced sexuality. For sixteen centuries Dioscorides' *Materia medica* dominated botanical thought, as the wisdom of the ancient Greeks remained accepted without question.

The Doctrine of Signatures, a popular philosophical-medical theory during the Middle Ages that relied heavily on superstition and myth, perpetuated the belief that orchids were synonymous with fertility and virility. Preparations from certain tubers were said to be effective in stimulating sexual desire, helping to produce male children, and so on.

The writings of Hieronymus Bock ("Tragus"), 1489–1554, furthered the orchid's reputation for arousing sexual appetites. He based his work on the

This illustration of *Odontoglossum triumphans* appeared in Lewis Castle's 1887 book, *Orchids: Their Structure, History, & Culture*. It was selected from an issue of the *Journal of Horticulture*. Widely collected in England a century ago, this genus has recently become popular again, and the varieties being produced are stunning.

theory that all living things originated from lifeless matter; orchis (since it was assumed that they were seedless plants) sprang from the seminal secretions that dropped from mating animals. In 1665 his theory was "confirmed" by the German Jesuit Athanasius Kircher in his *Mundus subterraneus*; he called orchis *satyria* and alleged that they grew in the ground where animals bred.

The first reference to orchids in the Western hemisphere is in the Badianus codex, an Aztec herbal of 1552. It depicts vanilla as being used as a flavoring, as a perfume, and in making a concoction called *tlilxochitl*, a lotion for health. The herbals of the Middle Ages and later—notably those of John Gerard and John Parkinson, published in 1597 and 1629, respectively—considered plants important only for their usefulness to man. In Gerard's *Herball*, orchids are called the female Satyrion because legend purported they were associated with satyrs. The plants were believed to be the food of satyrs and responsible for helping to arouse them to excesses. In 1640 Parkinson, London apothecary and royal herbalist for Charles I, in his *Theatrum botanicum*, said of orchids (which he called Cynosorchis) that they stimulated lust. Just as men lived in the belief that human destinies depended upon the stars, they also believed that plants exercised powers over the welfare of man because certain leaves, flowers, and seeds resembled parts of the human anatomy. Thus, if a plant had a leaf that resembled a human liver, it was said that it was intended as a remedy for hepatic disease. If the flower was heart-shaped, it would cure cardiac complaints.

It was not until the eighteenth century that botanical science was born and the first attempts at classification were made. The great Swedish botanist Carolus Linnaeus introduced systematic botany with his *Genera plantarum*, published in 1737. He placed orchids and other plants in classes founded on the number and positions of the stamens and pistils of the flowers. In 1753 he described eight orchid genera (retaining the name orchis) in his *Species plantarum*, which is still a reference source for botanical nomenclature. In 1763 another treatise by Linnaeus named a hundred different species, but all were placed in the same genus, *Epidendrum*.

Timeless beauty of form and decoration characterize this stoneware jar (c. 1650) of the Korean Yi dynasty. The representation of orchids here has a startlingly Abstract Expressionist quality.

Influence in China and Japan

The Chinese and Japanese were avid gardeners from the earliest times, appreciating plants for their beauty and fragrance as well as for their utility. The orchid had no particular importance as a medicinal plant but was grown for its fragrance and was also a favorite subject of painters.

Orchids were called *lan* by Confucius (c. 551–479 B.C.); he compared the flowers to the perfect or superior man and the scent of the blooms to the joys of friendship. (The word *lan* quite possibly referred to other flowers as well.) More properly, orchids were cited as *lan hua*. In a book by Matsuoka, printed in 1772 (rewritten in Chinese and quite possibly taken from the original Japanese book titled *Igansai-ranpin*, printed in 1728), six orchids were cited: *Cymbidium ensifolium*, *Angraecum falcatum*, *Cymbidium virescens*, *Dendrobium moniliforme*, *Sarcochilus japonicus*, and *Bletia hyacinthina*. Fragrance is indeed a great attribute of these plants, for I have grown five of the six, and a single flowering plant perfumes an entire garden room.

References to orchids in earlier books appeared as far back as A.D. 290–370, but these books treated orchids more in the botanical than the aesthetic sense. In the Northern Sung period (960–1279) there were special monographs on orchids, and the Chinese painters of the Yüan dynasty (1279–1368) were well known for their depiction of the plants.

Several orchids, including dendrobium and vanda, were mentioned by early Chinese writers, but the cymbidium was the most popular. These orchids were especially revered by Chinese painters for their grassy, graceful foliage, the tapered leaves and sculptural flowers being ideally suited to the calligraphic art of ink and brush. The painting of cymbidiums was very like the beautiful calligraphy of the Chinese; short strokes of the brush were used, simplicity was the style, and mood the ultimate goal. These are certainly not botanical drawings in the true sense of the word, rather, they are lovely, eye-pleasing pictures. There was no counterpart to them in European wood-block illustrations of herbals, where botanical accuracy and horticultural importance were stressed.

The most famous group of Chinese orchid paintings is contained in the treatise *Mustard Seed Garden Painting Manual (Chieh Tzu Huan Chuan)*, by Wang An-Chien and his three brothers. In this work the grassy foliage of the cymbidium is depicted in short, deft strokes in black and white, like a silhouette (a form called ink orchids).

Orchids were known and admired in China and Japan long before they were appreciated in Europe, and knowledge of them remained in the Far East. There was no exchange of plant information with the rest of the world. The Japanese found Christianity an evil, and they were intensely afraid of invasion by foreign powers. (When Western maps became available, the Japanese realized their country was small in comparison to the rest of the world, where many powers were engaged in wars of conquest.) In 1639, all foreigners were restricted to a man-made island called Deshima, in Nagasaki harbor, and a year later the only foreigners allowed were certain members of

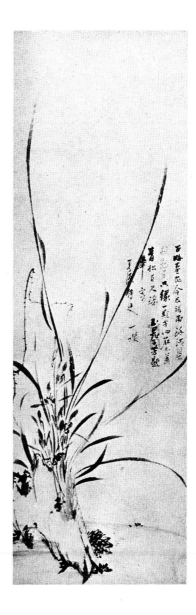

These graceful cymbidiums, painted by Gyokuen Bompo (1344–c. 1420), are found in volume 11 of *Genshoku Nihon no Bijutsu*, which is housed in Rokuo-in Temple, Kyoto.

the Dutch East India Company. Communication with European countries ceased, and only Asian ships were permitted to trade in Japanese ports.

First European Collectors

Systematic evidence of orchids in Oriental cultures appeared as early as the Sung dynasty (960–1279), but orchids did not begin to create interest in Europe until about 1750. The first European reference to Oriental orchids appeared in 1712 in *Amoenitatum exoticarum*, by Englebert Kaempfer, a German physician attached to the Dutch East India Trading Company. The first non-European tropical orchid, *Bletia verecunda*, flowered in England in 1733. It had been sent to a well-known collector, Peter Collinson, from New Providence Island in the Bahamas. The plant showed signs of life despite a voyage of several months. It was acquired by Sir Charles Wagner, and it flowered the next summer with clusters of small but bright magenta blooms. Because certain orchids could obviously survive in Europe (if conditions similar to their native habitat were provided), and because the West Indies (particularly Jamaica) were easily accessible to Europeans, naval officers started bringing more orchids home, either as botanical specimens or as gifts for their ladies. In 1760 *Epidendrum rigidum* was introduced, and in 1765 some vanilla species followed. Reports from the naval officers said that the plants grew to amazing heights, with their thick vines and aerial roots strangling branches and smothering trees. People therefore quickly tagged orchids as parasites—plants that have to prey on something in order to survive. This misconception about orchids was so persistent that in 1815 *The Botanical Register* confirmed it. (Actually, orchids are epiphytes, living *in* trees but not taking their nourishment from them.)

The first European to collect Asiatic orchids was Dr. John Fothergill. In 1778 he returned from China with *Phaius grandifolius* and *Cymbidium ensifolium*. He gave the phaius to his niece, and the plant produced an abundance of large, pinkish-blue flowers on tall spikes.

In August, 1768, the H.M.S. *Endeavour*, under the auspices of the Royal Society, planned an expedition to the South Seas for plant exploration with James Cook as commander and Joseph Banks as director. The first collection of plants was made at Tierra del Fuego in South America. In 1780 another expedition went to Australia and other places and brought back orchids.

Later Banks consulted with the king about the possibility of bringing breadfruit from the Pacific Islands to the West Indies as a commercial crop.

Banks was given permission and organized the journey. William Bligh was appointed to transport the trees and command the H.M.S. *Bounty*. The undertaking was a failure because of the well-known mutiny. However, in 1793, Captain Bligh was sent again on the H.M.S. *Providence*. This time he was successful, and from the South Pacific he brought back fifteen orchids including *Oncidium altissimum*, *Oncidium carthaginense*, *Lycaste barringtoniae*, *Epidendrum ciliare*, and others. Although each of the orchids that Captain Bligh collected were different kinds, they were all classified as belonging to the same genus, epidendrums.

Work progressed on orchids in other countries—Belgium, Germany, and France—but England led the way. John Lindley (1799–1865) started modern orchidology as we know it today. (Lindley, a professor of botany and Secretary of the Royal Horticultural Society, also edited the basic English horticultural journal, *The Gardener's Chronicle*, a highly respected periodical of its time.) In 1830 Lindley suggested growing orchids in damp, humid conditions; unfortunately, he based his suggestion on information pertaining to certain orchids in a restricted geographical location. The public at the time interpreted this to mean that all orchids should be grown in this way; the results were grave—thousands of plants perished. In Lindley's defense it must be stated that by 1835, with keener insight and more research on orchids in their native lands, he had determined that orchids grew at various altitudes and under a variety of conditions. He knew that the plants required different cultural environments. But the pattern was already set, and people continued to grow orchids in stagnant conditions. (Some orchids are, in fact, bog plants.)

Lindley wrote several books on general plant classification, but it was his work on orchids, primarily *The Genera and Species of Orchidaceous Plants* (1830–40), that brought him fame. Between 1852 and 1859 he produced *Folia Orchidacea*; though never completed it is a classic in botany.

Other notable men who contributed to orchidology were George Bentham, Sir Joseph Banks, Sir Joseph Dalton Hooker, Sir Joseph Paxton (gardener to the Duke of Devonshire), and B. S. Williams. Conrad Loddiges, James Veitch, and numerous others were also prominent in this time of "Orchidomania."

Though there was little correct information about growing orchids at the time, there were several periodicals that carried orchid data. *Curtis's Botanical Magazine* was started by William Curtis in 1787, *The Botanical Register* in 1815. *The Gardener's Chronicle* and Paxton's *Magazine of Botany* were other sources for orchid news. It was quite evident that the orchid was "the plant of the times" because so much was written about it in so many periodicals.

This illustration of the handsome *Cattleya loddigesii* is from John Lindley's *Monographia Digitalium* (1821). The species was discovered in Brazil in 1815.

In 1862, during the latter part of Lindley's career, the great naturalist Charles Darwin published *On the Various Contrivances by Which British and Foreign Orchids Are Fertilised by Insects*. The main part of the book discussed the morphology of the orchid flower, and it long remained a valuable reference work on plant-insect relations.

After Lindley's death Heinrich Gustav Reichenbach (1824–89) became the leading orchid authority in Germany; he identified and sketched species from all over the world. In other countries many notable persons were contributing to orchidology with various books and papers.

Indoor Gardens in England

Orchid collecting in England began with the flowering of the first imported specimen in 1733, as mentioned. Cultivation of exotic orchids for sale and in private collections began a little before 1800. In 1787 *Epidendrum cochleatum* bloomed in what is now the Royal Botanic Gardens at Kew, near London, and by 1794 there were fifteen different epiphytic (air plant) orchids in that collection, mostly of West Indian origin.

England in the early 1800s was a gardening nation, as it still is, and plants were most important in the English way of life. Orchids were unlike any flowers that had ever been seen. When a new plant bloomed, it was an exciting news item reported in periodicals and newspapers and by word of mouth. Orchids were considered oddities; it was said that they bloomed without soil and devoured insects in order to produce striking flowers. Bewilderment about how to grow orchids was justified, for no one knew what conditions they needed to flourish. Because they were known to come from tropical and humid lands, they were put in airless glass cases containing half-rotted tree stumps and branches. They were treated more as performing animals than as plants. Yet the curiosity persisted, interest accelerated, and more orchids were imported.

In 1815 Conrad Loddiges, a gardener and editor of a botanical journal, started to raise orchids successfully by unorthodox methods. He placed the plants in well-ventilated areas and watered them frequently; he kept them under glass but treated them as ordinary garden plants rather than oddities. They thrived. Other growers, too, started to experiment, some putting orchids in wooden or raffia containers and in sea shells. They gave orchids more ventilation and more light, and the plants responded favorably to this method of cultivation.

Loddiges, after this first success with orchids, asked William Roxburgh, the director of the Botanic Gardens in Calcutta, India, for plants and received species of vanda, aerides, and dendrobium. He began cultivating orchids for sale, and his work furnished considerable knowledge about how to grow the plants.

The first South American orchid to arrive in the Old World was *Oncidium bifolium*, which came from Montevideo. A traveler who brought back a plant said that it hung in his ship cabin and flowered without soil during the long journey. Although he was ridiculed by some for telling an outlandish tale, others accepted his story. And indeed in 1818, The Botanical Register confirmed his report, stating that some Asian orchids did bloom without soil.

In 1813 Fairbairn, a well-known gardener, was already having success with aerides and vanda species by growing them in suspended baskets and dunking them in water several times a day. By 1830 a more sensible treatment of orchids had started in England.

"Orchidomania" set in as the plants became fashionable. Social gatherings and parties were centered around the blossoming of an orchid; a craze gripped England that had no rival, not even the seventeenth-century "tulipomania" that caused financial chaos in the Near East and the Netherlands.

The orchid became popular both for its beauty and for the definite challenge of coaxing it to produce such beauty. Around 1840 collectors were sent in droves to all parts of the globe to find orchids to satisfy the public demand. The auction sales at Stevens Rooms, King Street, Covent Garden, and at other establishments were fraught with the excitement of a racetrack, and orchids were sold for sums incredible at the time. One cattleya sold for $600!

The clamor for and about orchids was heard also in Belgium, France, and Germany: at an international exhibition in Brussels, fifteen different cattleyas were shown; Belgian firms joined English companies in the sale of orchids.

Victorian Orchidomania

The orchid craze that started in England in 1840 and reached its peak in 1850 was the result of several influences. The desire for the flowers was not generated as it is now, primarily by their beauty. To the Victorian these plants were curiosities. The attraction of the bizarre and exotic was symptomatic of the times, but the practical contribution of one man, Nathaniel Ward, furthered the role of orchids as favorites of the era. Between 1830 and 1834 Ward perfected a closed glass-and-wooden case for shipping plants from foreign lands. The cases were not foolproof, but in them many orchids, rather than only a few, reached their destination. (Today, such glass containers are still called Wardian cases.)

As more plants came to England and more suitable ways of growing them were found, more people wanted them. In 1845 the repeal of Britain's glass tax and the general acceleration of industry made greenhouses or smaller glasshouses possible for many people. Furthermore, coal to heat the greenhouses was cheap, as was the labor to maintain them. As these "crystal palaces" appeared, so did unprecedented demands for plants to fill them, mainly orchids, for these were the gardeners' pet protégés in a world of great private gardens. By 1850 the English collectors started penetrating Central and South America, areas where exotic orchids grew in profusion. James Veitch, a nurseryman, sent William Lobb to South America to collect orchids. But perhaps the best-known collector of Central and South American orchids was Benedict Roezl, a Czech, who introduced many orchids from regions extending from Bolivia to the Atlantic and Brazil. No one knows whether he was luckier, more intelligent, or merely sturdier than his fellow collectors in surviving steaming forests and rugged terrain, but he furnished England with prodigious numbers of orchids.

Importation reached its peak in the 1850s, but four-fifths of the imported orchids died in transit, and no wonder. The penetration of jungles filled with insects and natives was only the first obstacle in getting the plants back to England: they then had to be packed into crates and transported by pack animals or by native bearers to a riverbank to await shipment, and often a boat did not arrive for weeks. Once on board they were stored in damp, warm holds lacking the two prime requisites of orchids, light and air. After a three- or four-month journey thousands of plants were found dead on arrival. But because they were rare, the demand for orchids soared and the supply was never enough.

During the mid-nineteenth century, orchid collectors also ventured into India, Africa, Java, Borneo, Indonesia, and New Guinea. Stories of their struggles drifted back to England and became magnified. One popular story of the time concerned a lost orchid, a cattleya that had died in an English collection and had to be replaced. But no one knew where it had originally grown! Such tales were common, and for forty or fifty years a species might be impossible to collect until a clue to its place of origin was found, often in some writings. A map showing a location for orchids had the value of a treasure map; collectors, in their zeal to look out for themselves, frequently

This illustration of a typical English glasshouse of about 1850 appeared in *Cranston's Patent Buildings as Applied to Horticulture*.

removed all traces of a stand of plants in its native habitat, or even forged maps to throw off rival collectors. A few plant hunters became very wealthy men, but many never returned to England with their treasures.

Stories of native tribes using orchids as religious and sex symbols were spread by collectors to glamorize the flower—the more unusual the stories, the more desirable the orchids became. Several orchids were actually used by native tribes in their ceremonies. The natives were dependent on their crops for food, and if by chance a brilliant mass of orchids bloomed about harvest time the natives viewed this as an omen: the orchids heralded a fertile harvest, and these people could not survive without one.

During World War I many fine orchid collections in Europe were destroyed or perished because of lack of fuel to heat the greenhouses. But in the United States such losses did not occur, and the popularity of orchids increased. Since the early 1900s private collections in the tradition of the English had been building, and orchids were starting to compete with roses as corsage flowers.

By 1930 the importation of orchids to England almost ceased because English firms no longer had collectors in all parts of the world. Nurseries were established in several tropical countries. In America and Europe great strides were being made in orchid hybridization, and plants were being cultivated on a large scale.

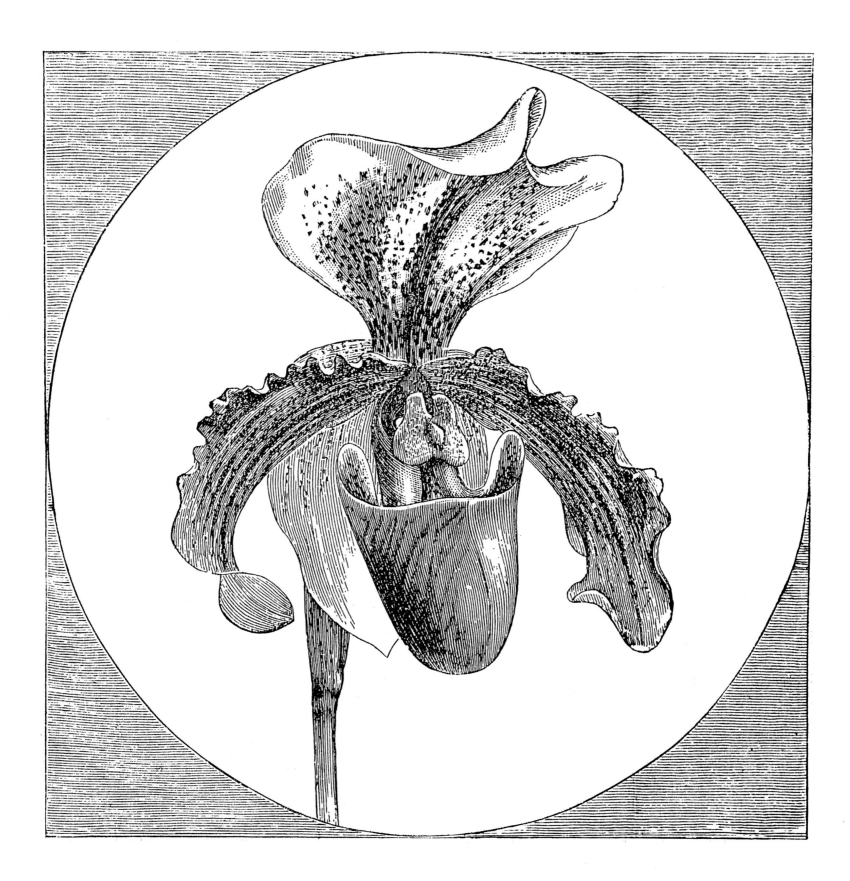

Botany

The Orchid Family

In the Orchidaceae we find one of the largest number of flowering plants known to man, with thirty-five thousand wild species and many thousands of registered hybrids. (The figure fluctuates as new hybrids are registered with the American Orchid Society and with societies in England and Europe.) Species—orchids untouched by man—grow wild in nature. Occasionally, natural hybrids are produced, but most hybrids are the work of man—the plants bearing the best (or certain desirable) characteristics are mated with other plants bearing other particularly desirable characteristics. For instance, a plant with large but poorly colored flowers might be mated with one which has small but beautifully colored blossoms in order to produce a plant bearing large *and* beautifully colored flowers.

Botanically, orchids belong to the system of flowering plants called monocotyledons. They bear a single seed leaf, or cotyledon, on germination; additional leaves are then produced from the center of the stem, passing outward. True bark is absent, and leaves generally have parallel veins, and the parts of the flowers (petals, etc.) in threes or in multiples of three. Dicotyledons, on the other hand, are distinguished by the production of two or more seed leaves on germination; the formation of young wood on the outer part of the stem; leaves generally with netted veins; and flowers with sepals, petals, and stamens in fours or fives or, in some instances, a multiple of those numbers.

Although iris, lilies, and amaryllis would also be identified by the above classifications, orchids have made such great advances in flower structure that the family appears unique among plants. With their intricate structure and ingenious methods of propagation, they function at the highest level of efficiency.

Called slipper orchids because of the shape of the lip, the cypripediums, now mostly known as paphiopedilums, have become favorite houseplants. This portrait of *Cypripedium Leeanum superbum* appeared in 1887.

Organization and Names

The divisions of genus and species date back to Aristotle's time, but for the last two hundred years taxonomists have used these terms with some modifications. As in the case of plant nomenclature in general, the orchid family is organized into a number of genera—the major ones are *Cattleya*, *Laelia*, *Oncidium*, *Odontoglossum*, *Vanda*, and *Ascocentrum*—each genus having one or many related species in it. Thus, orchids have two names, a genus and a species name. *Laelia anceps* refers to one specific plant and denotes that this plant belongs to the genus *Laelia* and is distinguished by the species name *anceps*. Plants belonging to the same genera have some characteristics in common. However, even orchids of the same species may vary in color and size, in which case a variety is recognized. Furthermore, even though *Laelia anceps* and *Laelia purpurata* are distinct species and may not look alike, they have enough characteristics in common to be in the same genus, which can consist of only two or three species or of several hundred.

Some of the best hybrids have been created by professional growers, but amateurs, too, have been successful in crossing orchids. Because of human curiosity and the desire to create something new, an infinite number of hybrids have appeared, and it soon became necessary to give a hybrid a name of its own rather than to call it by the name of a dozen ancestors. Thus, *Cattleya* Bow Bells × *Cattleya Edithiae* is called *Cattleya* Empress Bells. When an outstanding plant is introduced, a varietal name is added to the hybrid name and is set in single quotes, as in *Encyclia Mariae* 'Greenlace'.

In each hybrid group there may be many different clones, each with a clonal name and called a cultivar or variety (the terms are used interchangeably). The resulting name plant is given a varietal name in single quotes.

Award-winning plants from the American Orchid Society (AOS) or the Royal Horticultural Society (RHS) are often designated by initials after the name, such as *Cattleya* Mount 'Vashon' A.M. (Award of Merit) or F.C.C. (First Class Certificate).

All named hybrids must be registered by definite procedures. This is now handled by the Royal Horticultural Society of England. When the society receives plant data and information from the grower, the official hybrid names are printed in the English journal *The Orchid Review*. A compilation of registered crosses that are approved is published every three years and is called *Sander's List of Orchid Hybrids*.

With the crossing of so many different plants, some code names and abbreviations have evolved for the majority of hybrids that are produced by man. Cattleya hybrids, for instance, involve numerous successive crosses within a large number of species, each capable of contributing an outstanding characteristic to the ultimate offspring. Crosses are frequently made between laelia and cattleya and are known as laeliocattleya and abbreviated as Lc. Because of its handsome fringed lip, brassavola is extensively used in crosses with cattleya: these crosses are called brassocattleya and abbreviated as Bc. Frequently, three plants—laelia, brassavola, cattleya—are used and known as trigeneric crosses called brassolaeliocattleya, a real tongue twister shortened to Blc. Potinara is the code word for crosses that involve brassavola, laelia, cattleya, and sophronitis. Dialaeliocattleya has no coined name or abbreviation, so one must struggle with its pronunciation.

A final word about trigeneric and multigeneric crosses (hybrids produced from many genera) of orchids. This technique has been greatly accelerated within the *Oncidium* and *Odontoglossum* groups, and some incredibly beautiful plants have been created. New names have appeared on the scene, such as Odontioda, Odontodia, Renantanda, and Wilsonara. Some of these plants have become favorites, but others have been forgotten in the shuffle because not every cross is a good one.

Similar to other flowers, orchids may be known by their common names. These are often associated with animals and insects (for example, the butterfly orchid, the moth orchid, the bee or spider orchid, the cow-horn orchid, and the foxtail orchid) because the shape of the flower resembles a particular insect or characteristic part of an animal. Orchid names may also have religious connotations: *Peristeria elata* is the Holy Ghost orchid; in Guatemala, *Lycaste skinneri* v. *virginalis* is the white nun and *Epidendrum radicans* the crucifix orchid because of the shape of the flowers. The Mexican *Schomburgkia* (*Laelia*) *superbiens* is known as St. Joseph's staff and *Oncidium tigrinum* is the "flower of the dead" because it blooms on All Souls' Day and is used to decorate graves. Perhaps the loveliest name belongs to *Phalaenopsis amabilis*, known in Java as the moon orchid because its blooms last longer than a moon, a month or more.

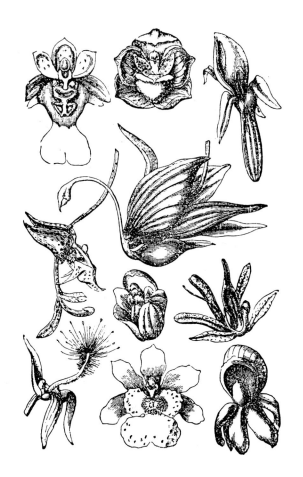

The various shapes of orchid flowers are illustrated here with examples of some favorites in England a century ago. This illustration appeared in John Castle's 1887 book on orchids. Among those depicted are the frog orchid, *Oncidium raniferum* (above left), and the swan orchid, *Cycnoches ventricosum* (center).

Orchids in the Wild

Contrary to what many people assume, not all orchids grow in steaming humid jungles. The majority are from the tropics, subtropics, and rain forests, but some also grow in temperate zones. Other members of the orchid family grow even in subarctic regions.

Calypso bulbosa, a bright magenta species, grows as far north as Finland. Lady's-slipper orchids are widespread in temperate North American zones, Alaska, and British Columbia, and orphys species are prevalent in Mediterranean areas.

In India the vast Himalayan mountain range is the home of many orchids—coelogynes, cymbidiums, and dendrobiums thrive at the various altitudes because the monsoon clouds from the Indian Ocean supply a tremendous amount of rain on the mountains' southern slopes. Orchids are well represented also in Burma, thanks to its clearly defined wet and dry seasons; the lovely *Vanda caerulea* grows at 6,000 feet (1,800 meters) in the Khasis Mountains of Assam.

The Philippines are rich in species, but perhaps New Guinea has more orchids than any other area, with approximately three thousand species. New Zealand and New Caledonia also have many orchids. The island of Madagascar off the coast of Africa produces dozens of angraecum and bulbophyllum species, for the warmth of the Indian Ocean and the extensive rainfall produce lush growth.

From the vast grasslands of East Africa come species of habenaria, eulophia, and disa, rare orchids seldom seen in collections. In West Africa, aerangis and polystacha plants flourish; close to the equator, in Sierra Leone, Nigeria, Ghana, the Ivory Coast, and Liberia, there are also numerous orchids.

Brazil produces species of cattleyas, laelias, and oncidiums, which are popular for corsages and as cut flowers. From southern Brazil to the Amazon in the north, there are plants of bifrenaria, brassavola, cycnoches, epidendrum, and zygopetalum, to name a few. As altitude and climate change, so do the orchid species, with certain types growing in rain forests and others in the damp heat of the Rio Negro basin of the Amazon.

The west coast of South America is as rich in orchids as Brazil. The Andes mountains, like a great snake, run the length of the coast and influence the climate and therefore the vegetation. In the Andes of northern Peru, masdevallias grow at 12,000 feet (3,600 meters) in freezing night temperatures. In Colombia, in the Andes region, the cool rain forests at 6,000 to 8,000 feet (1,800 to 2,400 meters) have large stands of odontoglossums and miltonias. Coming down from the mountains to the forests of Colombia native species of cattleyas may be seen, for example: *C. gigas*, *C. schroederiana*, and *C. trianaei*.

Venezuela is a land of contrasts, in weather as in customs. There are dry regions and rain forests, and in the northern mountains of the Cordillera grow oncidiums, cattleyas, and dozens of other genera; each area, dry, wet, or mountainous, has its own plants.

In a South American rain forest, a young boy collects orchids growing high on a tree.

In Central America we find veritable treasure troves of orchids in Panama, Guatemala, Costa Rica, Nicaragua, and Honduras. In Guatemala and Mexico there are assorted types of orchids at different elevations; some species are located in the cool mountains, others in the warm lowlands. Mexico boasts hundreds of orchid genera: laelia, oncidium, rhyncostylis, epidendrum, and so forth. Oaxaca, where I have collected orchids, is especially rich in species.

To appreciate the incredible range of orchids throughout the world, the native country of each species is usually identified in the descriptions accompanying the photographs.

How Orchids Grow

Orchids are diversified in their habit of growth; many live an arboreal life, others grow in the ground, some cling to rocks, and a few orchids can be called water plants. Most orchids are air plants, or epiphytes. They may use a tree or bush as support (but derive no nourishment from it), or cling to barren rocks or cliffs (these are lithophytic orchids). Some orchids, mainly those native to the temperate zone, grow in the ground like ordinary herbaceous plants and take their nourishment from minerals and water in the soil and obtain their carbon supply from the air. They manufacture chlorophyll through the normal process of photosynthesis like other green plants. These orchids can be identified by a prominent growth of fine root hairs, a characteristic that is not present in the epiphytic or lithophytic groups.

A few orchids are saprophytes; that is, they exist on dead or decaying animal or vegetable matter in the ground or on rotting logs and do not manufacture chlorophyll. These plants are impossible to cultivate when taken from their native habitat.

A few orchids are semiaquatics and grow in water, and two rare Australian genera, *Cryptanthemis* and *Rhizanthella*, are subterranean with only their tiny flowers appearing above the ground. There are also some leafless orchids such as those of the genera *Microcoelia*, found in Kenya, and *Polyrrhiza* in Florida, the West Indies, and Africa.

Although these are all distinct classes of orchids, the orchids themselves can, if necessary, sometimes adapt. A species that grows high in the trees may also thrive in the ground, and a terrestrial, if forced to, may take up life in the trees.

In the late nineteenth century Ernst Pfitzer proposed the first usable system of orchid classification, basing it upon the vegetative structures of the plants. Orchids that grew in one direction only were called monopodials; their stems lengthened indefinitely season after season and bore aerial roots. The flower was produced laterally from the leaf axils. The second vegetative class of orchids included the majority, and was called by Pfitzer the sympodials, plants in which the growth of the main axis or stem soon ceased, usually at the end of a growing season, and a lateral growth was produced in the next season. He further divided the sympodial orchids into two groups, and offered the third category of pseudomonopodial.

Taxonomists are always adding to proper plant classification as new research goes on. Thus reclassification of orchids takes place—for example *Brassavola digbyana* is now called *Rhyncolaelia digbyana*. Other changes in orchid nomenclature may be made by taxonomists because a species was described decades ago by authors who were unaware of other previously published names, or because they did not know the extent of the geographical distribution of a plant, or because of an original misidentification.

Flowers of the Four Seasons

Orchids have been called flowers of the four seasons because some plants bloom in spring and summer and others in fall and winter. As a reminder of the versatile nature of these plants, the season of blossoming is given in most picture captions. Generally, orchids bloom once a year and are quite dependable. Flowers are produced in a rainbow of colors, with perhaps yellow and brown predominating, as in many oncidiums and odontoglossums. Apple green appears frequently; ironically, lavender, the color of the popular cattleya, is not very common, nor is true pink. Scarlet, orange, blue, and virtually all other color combinations are found, except for true black, which does not exist. The so-called black orchid, *Coelogyne pandurata*, has a very dark green-purple lip. Colors may also be in pastel shades, delicate and gay, or they may be vibrant and bold, as in many of the hybrid paphiopedilums.

There is a remarkable range in the size of flowers and the texture. Some bulbophyllums and platyclinis species bear blooms less than $\frac{1}{32}$ inch (.8 millimeters) in diameter, but certain species of sobralia flaunt flowers the size of dinner plates. Some flowers have such transparent texture that you can almost see through them. Others, like ascocentrums, have sepals and petals that appear crystalline in sunlight, while another genus, the paphiopedilums, have a waxy texture.

Just as the flowers themselves are diversified, so is the method of bearing blooms. Many species have a solitary bloom on a short stem; others have hundreds of flowers on long sprays. Flowers may come from the base of the plant (as in the lycastes) or may appear on stems borne from the leaf axils (such as the angraecums and vandas). The stems may be pendent, reaching 6 or 7 feet (1.8 or 2.1 meters) long in *Dendrobium superbum*, or they may be stiffly erect, to 9 or 10 feet (2.7 or 3 meters) high in *Schomburgkia tibicinis*. Some trichopilias bear flowers that hug the pot rim, and acinetas and stanhopeas produce flowers on vertical stems 3 or 4 feet (.9 or 1.2 meters) long. (These plants should be in open baskets; in pots, the flower spike will often break the clay bottom to bloom!) Many cirrhopetalums and bulbophyllums bear flowers in a cluster of twenty or thirty tiny blossoms, a spherical bouquet that is an incredible sight.

Eighty percent of orchids are intensely fragrant. *Lycaste aromatica* has a scent of cinnamon; the odor of musk is easily recognizable in *Dendrobium moschatum*, while *Maxillaria atropurpurea* has a delicious scent of violet. *Dendrobium superbum* smells like rhubarb, and *Oncidium ornithorhynchum* is reminiscent of new-mown hay. Many angraecum and aerides flowers have a heavy fragrance much like gardenias, and *Brassavola nodosa* is so intensely scented that one flower perfumes a room. Mexican stanhopeas have medicinal (but not unpleasant) scents of menthol or camphor, most noticeable in the morning or early evening.

Most orchid flowers stay fresh far longer than roses or carnations. Cymbidiums are vibrant on the plant for two months; cattleyas last for a month. Many species of oncidium, cut and placed in a vase of water, last more than four weeks, and lycaste flowers are colorful on the plant for six weeks. A few orchids are short-lived: stanhopeas last a few days, and sobralias fade in three days.

The Orchid Plant

Most orchids used as houseplants have a feature called a pseudobulb. This is the swollen base of the orchid stem, which may be ovoid and a few inches long or cylindrical or stemlike and several feet high. It is almost like an above-ground tuber, and it acts as a storehouse of water and nutrients for the plant in times of drought.

The rhizome is the primary stem from which comes the secondary stem; it may be either elongated and leafy, or abbreviated and thickened into a pseudobulb. The form of the rhizome varies from genus to genus and species to species, and pseudobulbs also vary considerably in appearance.

Most garden plants keep their roots in the ground, and some orchids such as cypripediums grow the same way. However, as mentioned, many orchids are epiphytes; to get light they start climbing trees by using their stout aerial roots, losing contact with the ground. Many species have thick aerial roots that will cling to wood or metal surfaces. The ropelike roots can, in time,

THE ORCHID PLANT

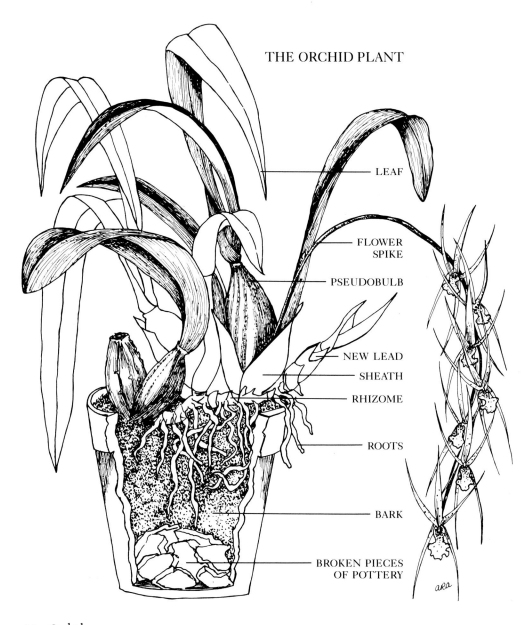

LEAF

FLOWER SPIKE

PSEUDOBULB

NEW LEAD

SHEATH

RHIZOME

ROOTS

BARK

BROKEN PIECES OF POTTERY

engulf their support so firmly that to take the plant from rock, stone, or wood, you have to cut it loose with an axe.

The diversity of orchid flowers is matched by the shape and color of the leaves. Some have foliage that hardly resembles leaves, such as *Brassavola nodosa* and *Scuticaria hadwenii*, with pencil-like cylindrical leaves, or *Isabellia virginalis*, which has leaves as fine as tiny hairs. The common succulent gray-green leaf of cattleyas and laelias may be ovate, subcircular, oblong, or elliptical. Leaves may be deciduous, semideciduous, evergreen, or semi-evergreen, depending on the species.

There are also little-known but intensely beautiful orchids that are valued for their foliage rather than for their flowers. These are called jewel orchids, and many have leaves with bronze- or copper-colored netting: *Anoechtochilus roxburghii* is a deep velvety green; *Macodes petola* is generally olive green, with contrasting veining; and the haemarias are a deep maroon, almost a rich black, with bright veins. These orchids look like beautiful tapestries and are unmatched in the plant world.

Mimicry and Sex

In most flowers it is easy to see the sexual organs—stamen and pistil, anther and stigma—but in orchids the anther and stigma are contained in one body, the column.

The flower of an orchid, which we love for its color and form, serves as a landing pad for insects that pollinate it. Charles Darwin understood the function of the orchid's sexual apparatus and described it in the treatise previously mentioned—*On the Various Contrivances by Which British and Foreign Orchids Are Fertilised by Insects*. His gentle Victorian readers might not have believed that the beauty of a flower was used for such vulgar processes.

Like other flowers, orchids have sepals and petals, three of each. One petal, usually much larger than the others, is called the labellum or lip.

The labellum, often the most conspicuous part of the flower, assumes an infinite variety of forms. It may be lobed, divided, or spurred; it may be slipper-shaped as in paphiopedilums, or trumpet-shaped as in other genera; it may have various appendages; it may be twisted or curved into complicated structures that recall old legends of the orchid's magical powers. The structure of the labellum, or lip, varies considerably in each genus, but its function is always the same—to assist in the fertilization of the flower.

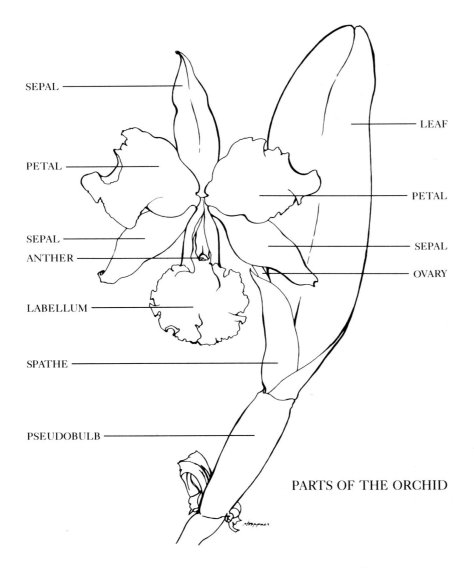

SEPAL

LEAF

PETAL

PETAL

SEPAL

SEPAL

ANTHER

OVARY

LABELLUM

SPATHE

PSEUDOBULB

PARTS OF THE ORCHID

The complex lips are really simple mechanical devices. Some, as in *Calopogon pulchellus*, are baited with imitation stamens, apparently loaded with pollen to attract insects. Others, as in *Coryanthes maculatus*, are bucket-shaped with a small quantity of water in them. Petals and sepals grasp the pollinator and drop him into the bucket; he emerges from the flower through tunnel-like structures and is loaded with pollen. In such ways the future of the orchids is secured.

The labellum may also form a lid hinged with a clawlike appendage. When the flower opens, the labellum turns around and falls back, covering the column and enclosing the insect. The device remains closed while the insect is inside, but if movement ceases, the lid soon opens again. The insect is freed, and the flower awaits its next pollinator.

Bulbophyllum barbigerum has a lip with layers of very fine hairs. At the end of the lip a delicate set of long purple threads waves in the slightest breeze, the constant motion attracting the pollinator. Many species within the genus *Pterostylis* have sensitive labellums: when touched by the weight of even the smallest insect, the labellum springs up to the column and imprisons the pollinator, dumping him into an intoxicating liquid. As he drunkenly staggers to make his escape, the insect carries off pollen.

Many orchids seem to mimic insects deliberately so that they can lure insect pollinators and thus ensure reproduction. The bee orchid, *Trichoceros parviflorus*, is a fine example. The male bee, thinking he sees a female, is attracted to the flower and is snared.

The highly sophisticated shapes and forms of the flowers serve to trap the pollinator once it is lured to the plant; scents and colors are other entrapments orchids use to ensure themselves a continued place in nature.

Many cypripediums lure their victims, usually flies, with a somewhat fetid odor. Others, in the genus *Cryptostylis*, are more subtle; their scent simulates the odor of the female insect. Coryanthes orchids drug their pollinators and then push them down an oiled chute into the flower, where they are drenched in pollen. When they recover, they crawl out to complete their role in nature.

By these deceptions orchids ensure their survival, and the appearance, smell, or shape of the labellum is matched to their selective system of pollinators. Often the flowers can be pollinated only by a specific member of a single variety of insect belonging to a single species. Such selectivity assures the plant of its continuation as a distinct species and reduces the chances of hybridization by crossbreeding.

L. *Satyrion Basilicum fœmina*.
Ge. *Handekenskruyt*.

Uses

Mythical and Practical Plants

Various parts of orchid plants have been used for centuries to make beverages, medicines, flavorings, and even magic potions. Most native Eastern orchids have tuberous roots filled with a nutritious, starchy substance that has a sweet taste but somewhat unpleasant aroma. For many centuries in Turkey and Persia a starchy meal was obtained from the roots of certain species of orchis and eulophia and exported as *sahlep* (salep). After roasting, it was brewed into a tasty beverage (it was sold in London before coffee supplanted it, and is still used in the East as a hot drink in the winter). It was also an efficient demulcent agent in herbal remedies. Prepared from dried and ground tubers mixed with water, salep is today used in various bland gelatines and soups. The succulent leaves of some orchids were formerly used as vegetables in Malaysia and Indonesia.

Witches were supposed to have employed orchid tubers in magic potions; the fresh tubers to promote love, the withered ones to check passions. In seventeenth-century herbals, as mentioned, orchis was called satyria, from the legend that orchids were connected with satyrs. In classical mythology, Orchis, the son of a satyr and a nymph, was killed by the Bacchantes; through his father's prayers he was turned into the flower that bears his name.

Aside from mythical associations and herbal remedies, the large family Orchidaceae produces only one product of commercial importance—vanilla (*Vanilla planifolia*). The vanilla orchid is a tropical, climbing, vinelike plant with large, oval-shaped succulent leaves and large, tubular yellow flowers. The Aztecs of Mexico were using vanilla to flavor chocolate long before the discovery of America. Vanilla was brought to Europe about 1500, but little progress was made in its cultivation. Most of the plants did not flower under European conditions, and those that did failed to produce fruit.

The name *Satyrion* was an early one for this orchis, but persisted, as can be seen in this illustration from Crispijn van de Passe's *Hortus Floridus* of 1614.

The similarity of the orchid's underground tubers to testes is shown in these illustrations from John Gerard's *Herball* (1597). From these drawings, it is evident why orchids have long been regarded as sexual symbols.

Vanilla was first successfully cultivated in Europe in 1807. In the following decades the development of artificial pollination, along with successful propagation from cuttings, made possible the growing of vanilla as a commercial crop throughout the tropics. Great Britain, Belgium, and France grew vanilla in several of their colonial possessions.

At present, vanilla is grown commercially in many countries, with Madagascar producing great amounts of the world crop. (Vanillin—artificial vanilla—was perfected in later years, and is now chiefly used in the baking trade as a substitute for the more costly true vanilla.) The plants themselves still remain difficult to grow. It is only recently that I have been successful with them, for they prefer a shady, moist, almost cool place. The mammoth yellow flowers have been well worth all my efforts.

The nutritive and healing properties of certain orchids have from time to time been employed throughout the world. Supposedly, natives in Madagascar make a scented restorative tea from the grassy leaves of *Jumellea fragrans*. Teas have also been made from the foliage or pseudobulbs of some species of renanthera and bletia. Roots of epipactis are used against arthritis in some regions and the flowers of gymnadenia as a preventative for dysentery. In Mexico, some laelias are used as fever cures, and *L. majalis* and

L. autumnalis are used in cough medicines. For wounds and cuts, the mucilaginous juice (salep) of the terrestrial orchid *Eulophia arabica* is frequently used.

In Chile some spiranthes species are prepared as a diuretic, and it is said that the bulbs of *Bletia verecunda* of Jamaica are boiled and eaten as digestive aids.

North American Indians used various ferns for medicine and food as well as the roots of some lady's-slipper orchids. These were boiled with a sweet liquid, and the decoction taken as a cure for headaches.

The flexible stems of some dendrobiums are used in weaving and basketry in parts of the Philippines and New Guinea, and intricate bracelets are made from the cane stems of other dendrobiums. In Brazil some natives use the mucilaginous sap of *Laelia autumnalis* as a glue in manufacturing musical instruments. In some sections of Central America the hollow pseudobulbs of Schomburgkias are made into trumpets and horns.

Orchids for Sale and Show

Today, as thirty years ago, the orchid is *the* corsage flower for special occasions. No flower is more beautiful for corsages than the orchid, and the public shows its admiration by purchasing millions of cut orchids annually for Mother's Day, anniversaries, and other festive occasions. Hybridization has produced mammoth blooms of incredible beauty that are hard to resist; though prices for corsages are still high, costs should decrease as meristem culture progresses.

Some commercial flower growers, such as the Rod McLellan Company in California and Orchids by Hausermann in Illinois, who devoted their growing space to sweet peas in the 1920s and gardenias and roses in the 1940s, now consider orchids their primary crop. In addition to cut flowers, retail plant sales constitute much of their business. There are about a dozen orchid suppliers who offer the cut-flower and plant-sales services in this country, and there are about one hundred mail-order companies that sell orchids to hobbyists and have no cut-flower operation. These companies have well-controlled crop-timing programs using shading, black cloth, or artificial lighting to produce flowers for the appropriate holidays of Easter, Mother's Day, and Christmas, and for the wedding months of June and July.

A typical orchid range such as Hausermann's has two hundred thousand producing plants under glass. Their annual marketable flower production is

42   Orchids

estimated at five hundred thousand blooms and increases yearly as does their mail order business of supplying plants to hobbyists.

Orchids are no longer just for the rich. The few private collections that once dominated the 1900s (the Rothschild in Europe, the Sherman in Boston) have been dispersed, given to public gardens, or sold to growers. In their place, thousands of more modest but superb collections of orchids have sprung up. However, a few private collections like the Du Pont orchids at Longwood Gardens near Philadelphia and the Fairchild Gardens in Coral Gables, Florida, have a wealth of plants for public viewing. The Brooklyn Botanic Gardens and the St. Louis Climatron also have extensive collections, and almost any conservatory in a large city has a sampling of plants. In England there are fine collections at orchid nurseries such as Armstrong and Brown, Black and Flory, Ltd., and Stuart Low Ltd. And the orchid collection at Kew Gardens has a worldwide reputation. The worth of the former private collections was no doubt staggering; on a lesser scale, for example, at an orchid auction in Belmont, California, about four thousand plants (a small number for a collection) sold for $27,000.

The American Orchid Society, with headquarters in West Palm Beach, Florida, has over twenty thousand registered members and over two hundred and fifty local orchid societies affiliated with them. There are chapters in most large cities, and some states have several orchid groups. There are several hundred other groups affiliated with the AOS scattered around the world. Amateur collectors number in the thousands.

There are shows, exhibits, and awards for growers in most cities at various times of the year, and of course new hybrids are being added to the official registered list every year.

Conservation

Years ago I saw a vast stand of native cypripediums in Wisconsin. On a subsequent visit to the same place, I found no trace of these plants. Whether environmental conditions had changed so they could not survive or whether the plants had been collected is hard to determine, but they were gone.

Generally, the situation of native orchids throughout the United States is the same: the plants are fast disappearing. Some states have passed laws protecting the plants, and other states will no doubt follow suit, but laws do not guarantee the survival of these wonderful plants. If the environmental

This massive interior of the government conservatory in Washington, D.C., shows the wide interest in exotic plants in America during the last century. Many of these conservatories were filled with orchids.

In Victorian England, most small greenhouses were of this size, approximately 18 feet wide by 40 feet long.

conditions are altered by pesticides and other pollutants, no restrictions against gathering the plants can save them.

Although we cannot legislate against parking lots and building developments—in general, the clearing of land for man's use—some restraints will have to be put into effect to preserve what we have. The answer may lie in part in the licensing of certain plant collectors, to reduce the danger of excessive collecting by individuals. Yet, to be fair, the responsible person who occasionally takes a few plants for his garden cannot in years do the damage to plants that one bulldozer can do in a few hours. For the time being, it seems wise to discourage people from collecting native orchids. There is no need for it. Today many suppliers can furnish pot-grown plants, and these generally are easier to grow in our gardens than wild collected species.

As Dr. Mark J. Plotkin has pointed out in his Foreword, in tropical countries where orchids abound, the preservation of native species is a matter of great concern. These include the orchids that are collected for sale to plant hobbyists. Some South American countries—Colombia, Peru, and Venezuela—have already put restrictions on native plants. In the African national parks for wildlife, native plants are given protection, too. Yet it must be remembered that plants can survive only *if the total ecological environment remains stable.*

For the most part, commercial cut-flower growers cultivate their own plants from seed or from the meristem process. Species orchids are also now being grown under cultivation. Although orchids are still collected in many tropical countries to supply growers, I see no real danger in this practice. Most commercial collectors in foreign countries are conscientious people who realize that only intelligent collecting will ensure plants for the future. And the recipients of these plants know how to care for them properly.

But the noncommercial harvest of orchids in foreign countries by tourists should, in most cases, be stopped. It is rare that the plants survive, since getting them established is one of the most difficult aspects of orchid growing. Conversely, the importation of wild species by the average hobbyist in the United States should also be stopped; the hobbyist may not know how to establish them, and this practice leads to wanton destruction of orchids.

In the 1930s the American public took African violets to its heart, and they became the number-one houseplants. By 1960 orchids had made inroads with plant hobbyists, and today the number of amateur orchid growers is fast surpassing that of African violet collectors.

The myth that orchids had to be sealed under glass to survive has finally been shattered. The misinformation that they needed elaborate equipment to help them grow has been erased. We now know that orchids can be grown as easily as many familiar houseplants. Their wealth of bloom and the drama of the flowers' growth entice people of all ages.

Cultivation

Living with Orchids

During the nineteenth century, orchids were encased in glass as if they were crown jewels and grown in greenhouses because they were considered delicate. Little did the people then know that the orchid is one of the world's toughest plants, determined to survive. In fact, orchids do survive without water and *bloom*, even if they have been neglected sorely for months. Today, thankfully, we know that orchids can be grown and can flourish indoors like any other plant. Indeed, under average home conditions, most orchids are more likely to thrive than the ubiquitous philodendron.

Many orchids have made the long journey from their native jungle habitat, and hybridists have produced myriad variations to beautify the home. Orchids are, without doubt, the houseplants of the twenty-first century.

Hybrids

In 1856 the first artificially produced orchid hybrid was perfected in England by John Dominy, head gardener for the Messrs. Veitch; he crossed *Calanthe masuca* with *Calanthe furcata* (the hybrid was named Calanthe Dominii). The early method of producing orchids from seed was called the symbiotic method; a host orchid or a specially prepared bed was used. The host plant was surrounded by a dressing of actively growing sphagnum, and seed was scattered over the compost and sprinkled with water. The special seed bed was prepared in clay pots and filled with sphagnum or chopped osmunda, and seed was sprinkled on top. The entire bed was then covered with glass.

The orchid craze of the 1890s in England spawned many conservatories where orchids were cultivated, such as this one, the Phalaenopsis house at Oldfield, Bickley. The wooden grid floor is still used in greenhouses today.

The Victorians doted on their plants, and sitting room windows such as these were common in homes. Today, the greenhouse window is their counterpart.

In 1922 the American botanist Lewis Knudsen substituted suitable chemicals for sphagnum or osmunda. A sterilized medium (usually agar jelly) was produced from seaweed, with organic and inorganic nutrients added and adjusted to a suitable degree of acidity. This was called the asymbiotic method of growing orchids and was used for producing most plants until recently, when meristem culture was introduced.

Recently, a yellow cattleya was created to tolerate low temperatures—40° F (5° C)—outdoors. This incredible development is only one small part of the brilliant work hybridists have performed to bring us the best in orchids. The hybridists' success has helped make orchids the number-one new houseplant in the United States. (Cloning, the other part of the story, is discussed in the next section.) Plants are hybridized to create improved plants with such desirable characteristics as better flower form, richer colors, more frequent blooms, and ability to grow in a wide range of temperatures.

More hybrids have been produced within the orchid family than in any other family mainly because of the great popular demand for orchids.

Cattleyas best exemplify developments in the field of orchid hybridization. Wild species untouched by human hands, such as *C. skinneri* and *C. forbesii*, are crossed with other wild orchids: laelias (known for their large flowers), brassavolas (characterized by fringed lips), and sophronitis (with a brilliant red color). Most of the cattleya hybrids have been created from crossbreeding with these three groups, or genera.

Extensive hybridization has been done recently with other genera—odontoglossums, oncidiums, cochliodas, and miltonias—to create trigeneric hybrids. Each genus contributes something unique to the ultimate sibling; such combinations take years to accomplish. When an outstanding cross is created, it is cloned. Thus, each plant is an exact replica (clone) of its parent.

Cloning

Approximately a hundred years after the first artificial orchid hybrid was produced in England, the revolutionary method of growing plants by meristemming started in France.

Meristem culture is now widely used in America. This process is faster and easier than earlier methods, and it ensures a faithful reproduction of the parent plant.

Every living plant has within it the tiny buds of new growths, a formative plant tissue made up of small cells and called the meristem. In orchid propagation a new shoot is cut off the mother plant, and several layers of leaves and tissues are peeled off until the meristem is exposed. The growing tip is then cut out (it is about a millimeter in diameter) and placed in a flask of liquid nutrient solution. The flask is then placed on a rotating wheel or vibrator, and within three to four weeks the meristem shows growth; tissue starts to develop into massy balls. In another month these clumps of tissue are cut into twenty or thirty pieces; each one is again placed in a flask of nutrients, and within a month these, too, grow about one fourth in size. (They can again be cut and returned to the flask for further agitation. The pieces follow the same growth pattern and can be cut again and again.) When the agitation stops, the small clumps start growing into plantlets that are then potted in seedling beds. The resulting plants are called "mericlones."

Orchids can also be reproduced by vegetative means—taking part of a mature plant to make new plants—an easy and effective way for the home gardener to get more plants. When a sympodial orchid such as a cattleya or laelia has more than seven or eight pseudobulbs, you can get a new plant by cutting off three or four whole bulbs with a sterile knife. Make the cut at the base of the plant where you see the connecting horizontal rhizome. Then pot each division separately.

Monopodial orchids such as vandas can be cut when they become too tall; cut off the top five- or six-inch (thirteen- or fifteen-centimeter) section and pot the new plant. It is as simple as that. It is a good idea to repot the parent plant at this time.

In 1961, Professor George Morel of the University of Paris perfected the first meristemmed orchid, an orchid created from the cells of another orchid. Morel used the basic technique first developed in 1946 at the University of California, in Davis, for other plants.

Meristem culture has reduced the price of the high-quality orchids. You can buy an exquisite red cattleya that previously might have cost hundreds of dollars for as little as $30. The meristem process means mass production: as the supply increases, the price goes down.

Producing plants from meristem culture is carried out by technicians in sterile laboratories. There are companies that specialize in this kind of work, and many orchid growers send their parent plants to these specialists. Some orchid growers perform their own propagation.

Orchids as Houseplants

With today's sophisticated home heating and cooling systems, orchids grow easily if they receive adequate water and nutrients. Today's home temperatures—generally 74° F (24° C) by day and 63 to 68° F (18 to 20° C) at night—are just right for most varieties of orchids. In fact, the nighttime drop in temperature is essential to the plants' good health.

Orchids do poorly in temperatures higher than 90° F (31° C) or in excessive humidity. If home humidity is 20 to 50 percent, most orchids will grow well. If it is more humid inside in the summer than in the winter, turn on a fan or the air conditioning. (Those old movies that showed orchids dripping water in fake rain forests were wrong!)

Ventilation is the area where most homes perhaps fall short, yet a free flow of air is necessary for good orchid growth. Few orchids grow in stagnant air. In the summer, leave the windows open if possible. In the winter, if you cannot let some air into the home when temperatures outside are freezing, use a small oscillating fan to keep air moving in the growing area.

Orchids make great indoor plants because they do not like or want intense sunlight. Some eastern sun is good, but hot western sun will quickly devastate orchids. The best situation is bright light, although certain orchids, such as most paphiopedilums, prefer a shady situation.

Always shade your plants from direct summer sun; even a light curtain at the window will help. If you are comfortable, your orchids will be, too.

If you are renting, you can still grow orchids. Generally in apartment buildings the heat is controlled by the landlord, and many times there is little heat at night in the winter. Your orchids will not keel over and die; if absolutely necessary, they can survive a few nights of very cold temperatures (50° F) (10° C).

Planting, Watering, and Feeding

Orchids do not grow in soil; they should be potted in fir bark, which is steamed bark of the Douglas fir tree. Fir bark pellets come in large, medium, and small grades. Hobby packages containing enough bark for four or five plants are sold at nurseries. Using bark is simple. Put pottery shards at the bottom of the container for good drainage; add the bark and tamp it down firmly so the plant is well supported. If the plant leans, put a thin bamboo stake into the bark and secure the bark and orchid with a wire tie. (Bamboo stakes and covered wire ties are sold at nurseries.) Some growers add peat moss, perlite, charcoal, and other fillers to the bark. Overall, medium-grade fir bark is fine for most orchids.

For years I have used five- or eight-inch-diameter (thirteen- or twenty-centimeter) terra cotta pots for my orchids. Plants grow well in such pots because the moisture evaporates slowly from the porous walls of the container, providing more or less even moisture for several days. But orchids can also be grown in plastic pots. Because plastic is nonporous, a potting mix in a plastic container will stay moist longer than a mix in a clay pot, which can be an advantage or a disadvantage. In warm climates, you can eliminate additional waterings if the mix stays moist. But in severe winter climates, lingering moisture can cause fungus to develop. Also, plastic pots are lightweight and can be top-heavy, so plants may topple over unless you put in enough ballast (gravel or shards) at the base of the pot.

The many different decorative jardinieres for plants are also fine to use; indeed, they show off orchids beautifully. However, it is best to insert an orchid growing in a clay or plastic pot into the jardiniere and fill around the

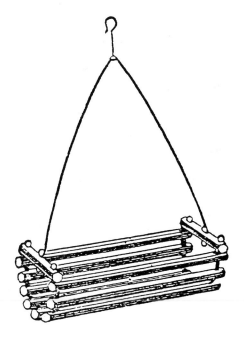

Teak baskets, with spaces between the slats to provide air from the bottom for orchids, are still used today as they were a century ago.

pot with decorative green moss. In other words, do not plant directly in decorative urns. The potted orchid in the jardiniere can be lifted out at any time. Always put a water-catching saucer at the bottom of a jardiniere. If the decorative container is on a table or other piece of furniture or on a wood floor, place a mat or piece of felt under it because a saucer alone will not prevent staining of furniture or floors. Water will eventually seep through and stain the wood.

If you can drink the water from your tap, it is safe for orchids too. If you live in an area with a high concentration of chloride and fluoride in the drinking water, let the water stand overnight in a bucket or watering-can so the chemicals can dissipate.

Cold water does not really harm plants, but tepid water is much better because it is less of a shock. Water in the morning so plants will dry out by nightfall; dampness at night helps encourage fungus disease. However, an occasional afternoon or evening watering will not kill plants. When you water, really water: get all parts of the mix moist. Let the water flow through the pot. Here is a general watering schedule:

Orchids in two- to four-inch (five- to ten-centimeter) clay pots: four times a week in warm weather; twice a week in cool weather
Orchids in four- to seven-inch (ten- to eighteen-centimeter) pots: three times a week in warm weather: twice a week in cold weather
Orchids in clay pots more than seven inches (eighteen centimeters) in diameter: twice a week in spring and summer; once a week in fall and winter

Contrary to much advice from other quarters, the practice of misting orchids can cause more harm than good. Water lodges in young growth and causes rot, and water accumulating on buds can cause them to drop off. Orchids do *not* need a rain-forest atmosphere. Adequate moisture in the air, about 30 percent, is all that is required to grow orchids. If your house is unusually dry and you must spray to increase humidity, spray the area surrounding the pot or use gravel in trays. Place potted orchids on plastic trays filled with one inch of gravel and keep the gravel moist, almost wet.

There are many, many plant foods for orchids on the market. I recommend the three I have always worked with and found very good for cultivating orchids (all are available at orchid suppliers): Peter's Orchid Food, Spoon-it, and Schultz. Schultz plant food is somewhat weak in nutrients for orchids, but Peter's works beautifully on orchids. There are two formulas: 10-30-20 promotes bloom, and 30-10-10 is for regular feeding. The first figure indicates the amount of nitrogen (for foliage growth), the second figure is the phosphorous (to promote healthy stems and flowers), and the third number designates the potash (to promote vigor). The food comes in the form of granules, which you mix with water. (The new time-released plant foods create havoc with my orchids, although they do work well for other houseplants.)

Do not apply any plant food when the fir bark is dry. Do not use plant food when the sun is shining on plants, and never try to force-feed a sick orchid. Whenever in doubt about any orchid, remember that it is better to feed lightly than heavily. My feeding program is as follows:

Orchids in two- to four-inch (five- to ten-centimeter) clay pots: standard plant food (30-10-10), once a month all year
Orchids in four- to seven-inch (ten- to eighteen-centimeter) clay pots: standard plant food (30-10-10) twice a month from August to January; 10-30-20 from February to August
Orchids in clay pots more than seven inches (eighteen centimeters) in diameter: 30-10-10 food once a month from August to January; 10-30-20 from February to August
Note: If winters are very gray, do not feed orchids at all during January and February.

This orchid, *Odontoglossum Alexandrae*, caused quite a stir when it was first introduced into England in 1863. It is still in demand today under the name *O. crispum*.

Promoting Bloom

There are three places to grow orchids indoors: at the windowsill, in rooms away from windows, and under glass in a greenhouse or in a garden room.

Windowsill growing works well at an east or south window. North windows are all right for certain shade-tolerant orchids, but avoid western exposures. Place plants on or in one of the many window devices: trays, shelves, or hanging units. Windowsill growing does *not* mean growing plants directly in the sill; it means near windows. Plants too close to windows may be harmed by severe winter temperatures or scorched by direct sun in the summer. Group plants at windows so they are easy to water and feed and you will not forget them.

Inspect and observe your orchids daily (you will do this almost by routine after a while), and if leaves are wan or yellow, provide more feedings. If plants refuse to bloom, increase the feeding program, with 10-30-20 plant food especially during the spring or fall, when most orchids bloom.

Always a favorite orchid, *Odontoglossum Pescatorei* is only occasionally seen in collections.

You can grow orchids anywhere in the home away from windows if there is good natural light. Orchids such as the phalaenopsis, paphiopedilum, and others thrive in such conditions—they become like any other houseplant, needing only routine care throughout the year. Once an orchid is in bloom, you can place it anywhere in the room and the plant will stay fresh for many weeks (some phalaenopsis flowers last three months!).

Greenhouse growing or a garden room situation suits many orchids, and many gardeners do have rooms devoted especially to orchids. This is a wonderful way of growing the plants, but it does require more of your time. Many plants growing together in a separate room must be observed routinely every other day. Proper ventilation is absolutely necessary—you must have a free flow of air and avoid crowding. Hanging plants from ceiling hooks or other hanging hardware enables air to circulate all around the plant. Growing conditions are much the same as for orchids near windows, but you will have to water and feed plants somewhat more often. Also be alert for any signs of invading insects.

More information about insect protection and orchids than is necessary is often thrown about. If you are caring for your plants reasonably well, there will be few or no insect or disease problems. Orchid leaves are just too tough for most insects, and because orchids are not grown in soil, insects and insect eggs cannot hide, but are clearly visible and can be eliminated.

If insects do somehow attack, do not panic. The three most common pests are aphids (oval critters that are easy to spot), mealybugs, (visible cottony white pests), and scale (brown or black insects). All these pests are easy to eliminate by applying standard rubbing alcohol on cotton swabs every other day for about ten days. Many plant books recommend chemical preventatives such as malathion, but I do not believe in using any chemical indoors.

Fungus diseases might attack, but they are rare. These infections cause a powdery, mushy growth and strike when many gray days in a row are coupled with damp and cold weather. The best defense against fungus diseases is to cut away infected parts and dust with powdered charcoal (sold at nurseries).

Virus disease is less a problem today than a few years ago because many orchid varieties are now disease-resistant. If you do see streaked or spotted areas (concentric rings) on leaves, remove the leaves immediately and discard them. There is still no dependable chemical preventative for virus.

People often ask me how to get orchids to bloom, and my answer depends on the type of orchid. Generally, a well-grown orchid will bear flowers, but as far as I know there is no surefire way to get stubborn orchids to bloom. However, I have learned a few tricks that will sometimes coax stubborn orchids into flower:

Cattleyas: Move them to the uppermost part of the garden room, or suspend them in hanging planters near windows.
Phalaenopsis: Decrease evening temperatures to about 58° F (15° C).
Oncidiums, Epidendrums: Move them about until you find a location they like. Sometimes an inch or two one way or the other can make the difference because of the different light and surrounding air flow.
Dendrobiums: Dry out plants severely for several weeks.
Paphiopedilums: Reduce watering.

Years ago, it would have been impossible to say that you could grow almost any orchid in this book, but today, thanks to progress in hybridization and in cultural practices, coupled with sophisticated heating and cooling systems of homes, much of this floral beauty is at your fingertips to enjoy. There are literally orchids for every occasion and for everyone.

There is something very rewarding in having blooming orchids from faraway lands at your windows. Like the armchair traveler, the orchid hobbyist travels great distances without leaving his home—the magic of orchids gives him a small window to the world.

So the lore and legends about orchids have dissolved as the cultivation of the plants has been understood. Yet the allure of orchids will always be there to capture the eye of the seeker of beauty.

The Orchids

More than 200 of the most typical and striking orchids are illustrated and described in the next section.

Notes about the Captions

Each caption consists of the orchid's name; for species, its place of origin; the common season of blooming; the flower size; and a comment. Regarding the localities, former or best known geographical names have been used for the most part. As to the size of a specific orchid, it may vary considerably, depending upon local growing conditions.

Organization of the Plates

The plates are arranged by genus and related varieties. The genera follow the order proposed by R. A. Dressler, whose system has gained wide acceptance since its introduction in 1974. Below, the numbers next to each genus and variety refer to the plates on the following pages.

Cypripedium

C. calceolus v. pubescens
North America, Europe, northern Asia
Spring
Flower width 1–2 in. (2.5–5 cm)

A native species with large flowers, it has sepals and petals of red-brown mixed with yellow. Occasional native stands are still found. It is very rare in nature and is an endangered species.
Plate 1 (left)

Paphiopedilum

P. insigne
Assam (India)
Spring/autumn
Flower width 3 in. (8 cm)

This is a popular, well-known orchid that has many varieties. The species was discovered by Dr. Nathaniel Wallich in northeast India. A terrestrial plant, it flowered for the first time in the Liverpool Botanic Gardens in 1820. *P. insigne* and *P. venustum* were the only two species of the leather-leaved group known for twenty years.
Plate 2 (opposite)

Paphiopedilum

P. praestans
New Guinea
Autumn/winter
Flower width 2–3 in. (5–8 cm)

An attractive orchid with leaves to 12 in. (31 cm) and large flowers. The twisted petals create a fantasy flower effect. The orchid was originally introduced in Europe in 1886.
Plate 3 (above left)

P. Maudiae
Hybrid
Winter
Flower width 3 in. (5–8 cm)

A stunning orchid, this winter-blooming plant prefers somewhat temperate conditions (75°F, 24°C). It excels in color and stamina with its flowers lasting for three to four weeks on the plant. An award winner, it is a cross between *P. callosum* and *P. lawrenceanum*.
Plate 4 (above right)

P. lowii
Malaya, Sumatra, Borneo
Summer
Flower width 3–4 in. (8–10 cm)

Discovered by Sir Hugh Low in 1846 growing high in trees, this species is still cultivated in choice collections. It was described for the first time in 1847 in the *Gardener's Chronicle*.
Plate 5 (opposite)

Paphiopedilum

P. micranthum
China
Variable
Flower width 2 in. (5 cm)

This unusual species was only
introduced about five years ago, and its
unique coloring has made it popular.
Plate 6 (opposite)

P. glaucophyllum
Java
Spring
Flower width 3–4 in. (8–10 cm)

This orchid was originally described by
the Dutch botanist J. J. Smith in 1900,
and later on, it was also known as
P. chamberlainianum. It is a prime
example of the exotic character of the
paphiopedilum flower.
Plate 7 (above)

Paphiopedilum

P. **Wineva 'Superior'**
Hybrid
Late summer/autumn
Flower width 4–5 in. (10–13 cm)

Another fine hybrid paphiopedilum with large blossoms of classic form. P. Wineva is a cross of P. Winston Churchill and P. Bourneva, made in 1977.
Plate 8 (above left)

P. **Farnmoore 'Rex'**
Hybrid
Autumn/winter
Flower width 4–5 in. (10–13 cm)

This favorite hybrid has an exceptional lasting quality, an excellent form, and an exotic color combination. The original cross was made in 1946.
Plate 9 (above right)

P. **Orchilla 'Chilton'**
Hybrid
Winter
Flower width 4–5 in. (10–13 cm)

One of the famous paphiopedilum hybrids, noted for its full rounded form and dark mahogany coloring. The original P. Orchilla cross was made in 1962 between P. Paeony and R. Redstart.
Plate 10 (opposite)

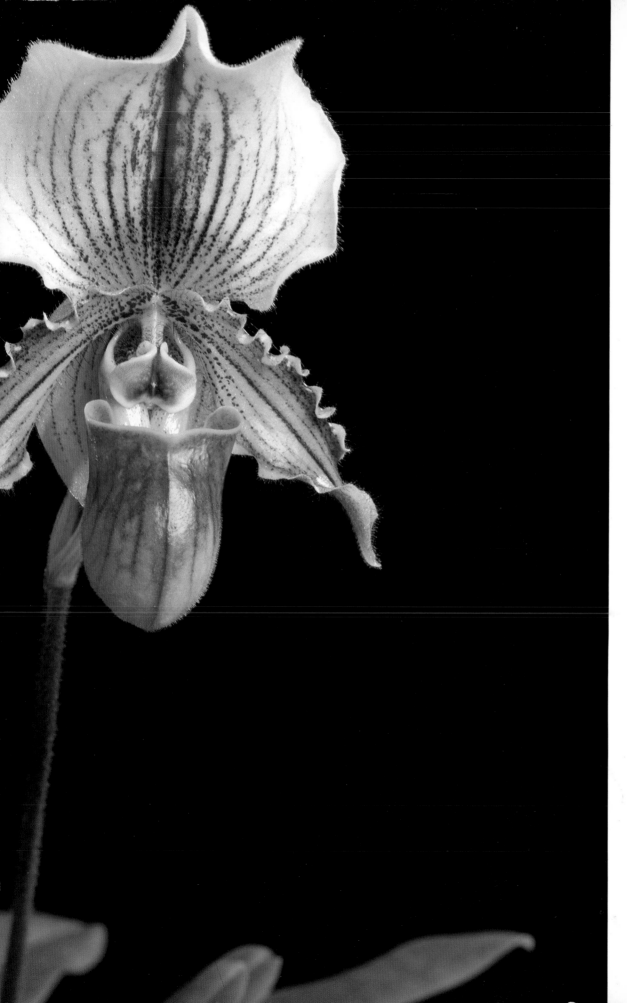

Paphiopedilum

P. Niobe
Hybrid
Winter
Flower width 2–3 in. (5–8 cm)

This hybrid cross between
P. fairieanum and *P. spicerianum* is an
inspired marriage, producing an
exquisite winter-flowering plant.
This orchid is highly prized and a
worthwhile addition to any collection.
Plate 11

Paphiopedilum

P. parishii
Burma, Thailand, China
Autumn/winter
Flower width 3–4 in. (8–10 cm)

This orchid was found in Burma in 1859 and was described in the *Gardener's Chronicle* in 1869. The orchid has a unique beauty coupled with exquisite form. The plant bears a strong resemblance to *P. lowii* and *P. philippinense.*
Plate 12 (left)

P. Bell O' Ireland
Hybrid
Autumn/winter
Flower width 4–5 in. (10–13 cm)

Another attractive paphiopedilum cross, this orchid was developed in 1980, a cross between Yerba Buena and Sheila Hanes. The pale green color is unusual for the *Paphiopedilum* genus.
Plate 13 (above)

Paphiopedilum

P. insigne* v. *sanderae
Assam (India)
Spring
Flower width 3 in. (8 cm)

Variety *sanderae* is superior to the
species in color and form.
Plate 14

Calopogon

C. pulchellus
North America
Spring
Flower width 1–2 in. (2.5–5 cm)

With its pale tufted lip and gracefully upturned petals, this orchid is strikingly distinctive in form. The genus comprises four species of hardy, terrestrial orchids that are mostly native to the southeastern United States, with one species found also in eastern Canada. This orchid is considered an endangered species.
Plate 15 (opposite)

Spiranthes
(Stenorrhynchus)

S. speciosa
Cuba, Jamaica, Puerto Rico, Guatemala, south to Colombia and Venezuela
Autumn
Flower width ½ in. (1 cm)

With rosettes of handsome dark-green leaves, this select form of the species has flowers on long stalks. The plant grows, blooms, and then rests for a few months before it repeats its cycle.
Plate 16 (right)

Polyrrhiza

P. lindenii
Southern Florida, West Indies
Spring
Flower width ½ in. (1 cm)

This is a leafless orchid that resembles
an insect more closely than a flower.
Its flowers are showy, fragrant, and
long-lived.
Plate 17 (right)

Stenoglottis

S. longifolia
Natal
Autumn
Flower width ¼–½ in. (.6–1.2 cm)

This epiphytic or terrestrial orchid has
a rosette of apple-green leaves and
was brought into cultivation in 1889.
A genus consisting of at least three
species, it has no known hybrids
as its genetic affinities have not
been deduced.
Plate 18 (far right)

Acanthophippium
(Acanthephippium)
~~~~~~~~~~~~~~~~~~~~~~

A. mantinianum (montanus)
The Philippines
Summer
Flower width 1–2 in. (2.5–5 cm)

With fragrant tulip-shaped flowers, this
is a rare terrestrial orchid allied to the
genus *Phaius*. The author's plant
blooms yearly in his garden room, after
a winter dormancy.
Plate 19 (above)

Chysis
~~~~~~~~~~~~~~~~~~~~~~

C. laevis
Mexico to Costa Rica
Spring
Flower width 3–5 in. (8–13 cm)

This species has long pendent stems
with papery-thin green leaves. It was
introduced from Mexico by G. Barker
of Springfield near Birmingham,
England, in whose collection it
flowered for the first time in 1840.
Plate 20 (right)

Phaius

P. tankervilliae (grandifolius)
China, tropical Asia, Australia
Spring
Flower width 3–4 in. (8–10 cm)

Brought from China about 1778 by
Dr. John Fothergill, this was one of the
earliest tropical orchids in British
collections. A terrestrial plant, it
produces erect spikes bearing many
flowers.
Plate 21

Phaius

P. Gravesii
Hybrid
Variable
Flower width 3–4 in. (8–10 cm)

A cross obtained by N. C. Cookson between *P. grandifolius* and *P. wallichii*, it flowered first in the collection of H. Graves of Orange, New Jersey, and it was dedicated to him. *Phaius* is Greek for swarthy, pertaining to the yellow-brown color of the flower. Plate 22

Phaius

P. maculatus
Northern India, Japan
Summer
Flower width 3–4 in. (8–10 cm)

Tall, to 40 in. (1.2 m) in height, and showy, this robust species was first introduced about 1822. The foliage is atypical among orchids; it is of rather thin texture and decorated with yellow spots.
Plate 23 (opposite)

Barkeria

B. spectabilis
Mexico, Guatemala
Summer
Flower width 2–3 in. (5–8 cm)

This Central American orchid is sometimes known as B. Lindleyana. Originally called an *Epidendrum*, it was transferred to the *Barkeria* genus in 1849. Originally introduced in Europe in 1842, it first bloomed at the Royal Horticultural Society.
Plate 24 (above left)

B. skinneri
Guatemala
Summer
Flower width 2–3 in. (5–8 cm)

These plants are deciduous, losing their leaves during their season of rest. The flowers are a striking color. The species is now often included in the genus *Epidendrum*. First described in the *Magazine of Botany* in 1849, it is now extinct in its natural habitat.
Plate 25 (above right)

Brassavola

B. glauca v. alba
Mexico
Summer
Flower width 5–7 in. (13–18 cm)

B. glauca was first described in 1839 in the *Botanical Register*; this rare form of *B. glauca* with its over-sized flowers is almost pure white. It was first introduced as *Laelia glauca*.
Plate 26

Brassavola

B. *digbyana*
Honduras
Summer
Flower width 6–7 in. (15–18 cm)

Because of its beautiful fringed lip,
this orchid is used extensively for
hybridization. The blossom is
unusually large for an orchid, and the
scent is exquisite and powerful.
Though a difficult plant to coax into
bloom, the effort required produces
results that are well worth the trouble.
Today, this species is hard to find
in its native habitat because of its
desirability to collectors and hybridists.
Plate 27 (opposite)

B. *nodosa*
West Indies, Mexico through Central
America to Venezuela and Peru
Variable
Flower width 2–3 in. (5–8 cm)

Known as lady-of-the-night, this orchid
(in the foreground) is sweetly scented
and small in stature. The original wild
species was described in 1735 as
Epidendrum nodosum. It practically
grows by itself. In the background are
blossoms of the standard form of
Dendrobium phalaenopsis.
Plate 28 (right)

Cattleya

C. Princess Bells
Hybrid
Variable
Flower width 3–4 in. (8–10 cm)

An exceptionally fine orchid, it is a
cross between C. Bob Betts and
C. Empress Bells. The stud, C. Bob
Betts, is one of the finest white-
flowered orchids in existence.
Plate 36

Cattleya

~~~~~~~~~~~~~~~~~~~~~~~~~~~~~~~~~~~~~~

C. Landate
Hybrid
Variable
Flower width 3–4 in. (8–10 cm)

A primary hybrid between the species
C. guttata and *C. aclandiae*, this fine
orchid has both color and form. The
original cross was made in 1966.
Plate 37 (opposite)

~~~~~~~~~~~~~~~~~~~~~~~~~~~~~~~~~~~~~~

C. granulosa
Guatemala, Brazil
Summer
Flower width 3 in. (8 cm)

While this fine orchid is attributed
to Guatemala and Brazil, its origins
are unclear; explorers may have
deliberately given misleading locations
to protect the bounty. It was
introduced into Europe around 1840.
Plate 38 (right)

Cattleya

C. loddigesii × **C. luteola**
Hybrid
Summer/autumn
Flower width 4–5 in. (10–13 cm)

C. loddigesii was the first cattleya introduced into Europe; it came from Rio de Janeiro and was first classified as an epidendrum. *C. luteola* is a dwarf orchid brought into cultivation about 1853. These two magnificent cattleyas combine to create this delicately-colored, stunning orchid.
Plate 39

Cattleya

C. amethystoglossa v. rosea
Hybrid
Spring
Flower width 4–5 in. (10–13 cm)

C. amethystoglossa is allied to *C. guttata* and *C. leopoldii* but the sepals are pale pink and the petals have some dark purple spots. The flowers are borne in clusters. This variety is somewhat darker in color than the original species.
Plate 40

C. labiata v. coerulea
Hybrid
Variable
Flower width 4–5 in. (10–13 cm)

C. labiata was the first single-leaved cattleya species with large flowers to be discovered. This fine hybrid is a recent cross to produce an orchid that is almost blue in color.
Plate 41

Cattleya

C. velutina
Brazil
Summer
Flower width 3–5 in. (8–13 cm)

Introduced into cultivation about 1872,
this species first flowered in England
under J. Broome in Didsbury,
Manchester. The plant is similar to
C. bicolor, and was once known as
C. fragrans. The plant is tall, growing
to 60 in. (1.5 m) and has very fragrant
flowers.
Plate 42

Cattleya

〰〰〰〰〰〰〰〰〰〰〰〰〰〰〰〰

C. walkeriana
Brazil
Winter
Flower width 3–4 in. (8–10 cm)

Collected in 1839–40 and named after
Edward Walker, this orchid is a rather
small plant, growing only up to 12 in.
(33 cm) tall but bearing large solitary
flowers. Discovered by G. Gardner and
also M. Libon, a collector who sent
plants to M. Galeotti in Belgium in
1848.
Plate 43 (left)

〰〰〰〰〰〰〰〰〰〰〰〰〰〰〰〰

C. Frasquita
Hybrid
Variable
Flower width 3 in. (8 cm)

A hybrid made originally in 1900, it is a
cross between the species *C. bicolor*
and *C. velutina*. The plant grows to 60
in. (1.5 m) tall, and the handsome
flowers are easily brought into bloom.
Plate 44 (opposite)

Cattleya

∿∿∿

C. Chocolate Drop 'Kodana'
Hybrid
Autumn
Flower width 2–3 in. (5–8 cm)

An unusual dwarf-type cattleya with waxy, textured flowers, this orchid, a cross of *C. guttata* and *C. aurantiaca*, was introduced in 1955 and has become quite popular as a novelty orchid.
Plate 45 (opposite)

C. amethystoglossa 'Berwicks'
Hybrid
Summer/autumn
Flower width 4 in. (10 cm)

This is a superior form of the species (see plate 34) and excels in color.
Plate 46 (above left)

C. dowiana v. *aurea*
Costa Rica, Colombia
Autumn
Flower width 4 in. (10 cm)

This was first discovered in 1847, decades before 'Orchidomania' seized Great Britain. The usual color is yellow flecked with crimson, but, here in the rare white form, the sepals and petals have no crimson marking, and the lip has more yellow.
Plate 47 (above right)

Brassocattleya

Bc. Star Ruby 'Craig'
Hybrid
Summer/autumn
Flower width 1–2 in. (2.5–5 cm)

An unusually small orchid for a
cattleya, its flowers are noted for their
vivid color. The original cross, made
by W.W.G. Moir in 1945, was
Brassavola nodosa × *Cattleya batalinii*.
Plate 48 (above)

Bc. Maikai 'Mayumi'
Hybrid
Variable
Flower width 2–3 in. (5–8 cm)

This cross between brassavola and
cattleya produced a fine miniature
cattleya with distinctive lavender
flowers. It was awarded the Highly
Commended Certificate from the
American Orchid Society (HCC/AOS).
Plate 49 (opposite)

Sophrolaeliocattleya

Slc. Jewel Box 'Dark Waters'
Hybrid
Late winter
Flower width 5–6 in. (13–15 cm)

A hybrid in the red family of colors (sophronitis, laelia, and cattleya), this stunning orchid displays its vigorous blossoms soon after the New Year. A mature plant can have as many as 50 to 60 individual flowers. Slc. Jewel Box is a cross between *C. aurantiaca* and *C.* Anzac.
Plate 65

Coelogyne

C. pandurata
Borneo
Summer
Flower width 2–3 in. (5–8 cm)

This is the "legendary" black orchid, found in Hollywood movies. The stained lip is actually a deep blackish green, not a true black. The plant bears magnificent flowers that capture the eye of even the nongardener.
Plate 66 (above)

C. ochracea
India
Spring/summer
Flower width 2–3 in. (5–8 cm)

A pretty orchid that is also easy to grow, it was originally introduced into culture about 1846.
Plate 67 (right)

Coelogyne

C. lawrenceana
Vietnam, Burma
Summer
Flower width 4 in. (10 cm)

A fine epiphytic species, it has two-leaved, oval pseudobulbs and large, waxy, fragrant flowers borne on an erect stalk. This is an orchid of true elegance and grace, first collected in Burma about 1854.
Plate 68 (left)

Epidendrum (Encyclia)

E. Mariae 'Greenlace'
Mexico
Summer
Flower width 3–4 in. (8–10 cm)

Found at high elevations, E. Mariae is a small plant, almost a dwarf in height—to about 12 to 14 in. (30 to 36 cm). The superior form 'Greenlace' has pronounced green coloring. This orchid was awarded the Certificate of Cultural Merit by the American Orchid Society (CCM/AOS).
Plate 69 (opposite)

Epidendrum

E. wallisii
Panama, Colombia
Autumn/winter
Flower width 1–2 in. (2.5–5 cm)

This beautiful orchid bears waxy, long-lived fragrant flowers. It was first discovered in 1874. H. G. Reichenbach described it in the *Gardener's Chronicle* in 1875.
Plate 70 (below left)

E. tampense
Bahamas, Florida
Spring/summer
Flower width ½–1 in. (1 cm)

Generally found in Florida, this wild flower is a free flowering plant that bears a profusion of flowers that are both fragrant and long-lived.
Plate 71 (below right)

E. prismatocarpum
Costa Rica
Summer/autumn
Flower width 1–2 in. (2.5–5 cm)

A very desirable plant, this robust orchid has long scapes of small beautiful, waxy flowers, lasting for several weeks. The species name refers to the three sharp angles of the short ovary. The orchid was discovered by Jósef Warscewicz around 1849.
Plate 72 (opposite)

Epidendrum

E. stamfordianum
Mexico to Panama, Colombia,
Venezuela
Spring
Flower width ½–1 in. (1–2.5cm)

This handsome species, producing
long, arching stems, was discovered by
G. Ure Skinner in Guatemala in 1837.
It was sent to James Bateman of
Knypersley, England, where it
flowered in the spring of the following
year.
Plate 73

Epidendrum

E. nemorale
Mexico
Spring
Flower width 1–3 in. (2.5–8 cm)

With egg-shaped pseudobulbs and
stems growing to about 20 in. (51 cm)
tall, this epidendrum was first
imported by Conrad Loddiges from
Mexico about 1840. It is a tree dweller
often seen in the regions around
Oaxaca. The flowers are scented and
remain in color for six weeks on
the plant.
Plate 74 (opposite)

E. atropurpureum
Central and South America
Spring
Flower width 2½ in. (6 cm)

First discovered by F.H.A. von
Humboldt and Aimé J. A. Bonpland in
Venezuela about 1836, this is an orchid
that is distributed over an especially
wide range. The flowers are possibly
the largest in the genus.
Plate 75 (above)

Epidendrum

E. radicans
Guatemala, Mexico
Summer/autumn
Flower width ½–1 in. (1–2.5 cm)

This reed-stemmed orchid from a temperate climate will flourish in the garden. Discovered by G. Ure Skinner in 1837, it was sent to the Royal Horticultural Society of London. It bloomed for the first time in the collection of Mrs. Lawrence at Ealing.
Plate 76 (left)

Laelia

L. flava
Brazil
Spring
Flower width 1–2 in. (2.5–5 cm)

Introduced into English collections in 1839, this lovely epiphytic orchid has small, elegant, golden flowers. It is said to be the first yellow, miniature laelia discovered.
Plate 77 (opposite)

136 Laelia

Laelia

L. tenebrosa
Brazil
Summer
Flower width 7–8 in. (18–20 cm)

This plant is 30 in. (76 cm) tall, with
large flowers. A magnificent sight in
bloom, it can tolerate a variety of
temperatures from 55°F to 80°F (12°C
to 26°C). It was first described in
1893 in the *Orchid Review*.
Plate 78 (opposite)

L. superbiens
Mexico, Guatemala
Winter
Flower width 7–8 in. (18–20 cm)

Discovered by G. Ure Skinner in
1838–39 in Honduras and introduced
into England in 1844, *L. superbiens*
is an unusual plant. It has large
pseudobulbs and bears a 4-foot
(1.2–meter) flower spike crowned with
clusters of blooms. The plant is a sun-
lover and not easy to bring into bloom.
It is also called *La vera del Señor San
José*, the wand of St. Joseph, referring
to the long flower spike.
Plate 79 (right)

Laelia

~~~~~~

L. purpurata
Brazil
Summer
Flower width 6–7 in. (15–18 cm)

This fine species is distinguished
by handsome, large flowers veined
with amethyst purple. It was first
discovered in 1847 in southern Brazil.
Plate 80 (above)

L. cinnabarina
Brazil
Winter/spring
Flower width 5–6 in. (13–15 cm)

This species was introduced into
England by Messrs. Young,
nurserymen, in 1836. It is a medium-
size plant, to 24 in. (61 cm) tall.
A favorite with hobbyists, it is
spectacular in flower, easy to cultivate,
and is a dependable bloomer. Pictured
here is a select form of the species.
Plate 81 (right)

Laelia

L. anceps 'Roeblingiana'
Hybrid
Late summer/early autumn
Flower width 7–8 in. (18–20 cm)

This orchid is derived from a Mexican species, *L. anceps*, which was introduced in 1835 and had been a popular orchid for decades. The huge flower with its pointed petals has exceptional grace.
Plate 82 (above right)

L. perrinii
Brazil
Winter
Flower width 4–5 in. (10–13 cm)

This orchid was described in *Paxton's Magazine of Botany* in 1847. It has fine form and the long-lasting quality of flowers common to most laelias.
Plate 83 (below right)

Leptotes

L. bicolor 'Karem'
Hybrid
Summer
Flower width 3–4 in. (8–10 cm)

The original species is miniature in size and was first discovered in the Organ Mountains by Mrs. Arnold Harrison of Liverpool in 1831 or 1832. Afterward, G. Gardner sent the species to the Woburn Abbey Collection, in England, where it flowered for the first time in 1839.
Plate 84 (opposite)

Masdevallia

M. strobelii × ***M. coccinea***
Hybrid
Winter/spring
Flower width 1 in. (2.5 cm)

A miniature to dwarf epiphyte,
M. strobelii is a charming plant for
the windowsill. The cross with
M. coccinea results in a reddish pattern
on the petals.
Plate 85 (left)

***M. infracta* 'Devine'**
Hybrid
Spring
Flower width 2 in. (5 cm)

'Devine' is a superior form of the
original species which is from Brazil or
Peru. It was discovered in the early
1800s by the French traveler and
naturalist Michael Descourtilz, who
found it growing on the wooded
mountains which separate Rio de
Janiero from the Campos. G. Gardner
gathered the plant in the Organ
Mountains in 1837, and he sent it to
Messrs. Loddiges in England. The
American Orchid Society awarded this
orchid its Certificate of Cultural Merit
(CCM/AOS).
Plate 86 (opposite)

Masdevallia

M. coccinea v. Harryana
Peru
Spring
Flower width 1–2 in. (2.5–5 cm)

Introduced in 1871 from the Andes
Mountains, this orchid is more
desirable than *M. coccinea*, having
better color and form. The unusual
flower shape (resembling a kite) is
uncommon in the orchid world.
Plate 87 (left)

M. coccinea 'Jessica's Delight'
Hybrid
Winter/spring
Flower width 1–2 in. (2.5–5 cm)

The original species is from Colombia
and Peru. A fine orchid, *M. coccinea*
was originally brought into cultivation
about 1846.
Plate 88 (above)

Masdevallia

M. amabilis
Northern Peru
Winter
Flower width 1–2 in. (2.5–5 cm)

This breathtaking orchid has dramatic
flowers. The plant is small, to 6 in.
(15 cm) tall, with a wiry stem, bearing
a solitary flower. First discovered by
Jósef Warscewicz in 1850, it was not
cultivated until 1872 in London.
Plate 89

M. veitchiana
Peru
Winter/spring
Flower width 2–3 in. (5–8 cm)

This orchid comes from the high
country of the Andes looking less like
an orchid than like a colorful kite.
The plant was discovered by R. W.
Pearce in the Andes and introduced in
1867 by James Veitch and Sons. The
leaves are only 5 to 6 in. (13 to 15 cm)
long with small flowers borne on long
20-in. (51-cm) stems.
Plate 90

Pleurothallis

P. grobyii
Mexico and South America
Variable
Flower width ¼–½ in. (.5–1 cm)

This is a common orchid. It came into
cultivation about 1835. It was first
described by John Lindley in the
Botanical Register. The plant was
cultivated by Messrs. Loddiges of
Hackney, London. Named in honor of
Lord Grey of Grobyi, who was an
ardent orchid grower.
Plate 91

Sophronitis

~~~~~~~~~~~~~~~~~~~~~~

S. *coccinea*
Brazil
Summer/autumn
Flower width 4 in. (10 cm)

This superlative epiphytic or
lithophytic orchid, a true miniature,
was originally called a cattleya when
documented by John Lindley in the
Botanical Register in 1836. H. G.
Reichenbach put it into its proper
category in 1864.
Plate 92 (above)

Dendrobium

~~~~~~~~~~~~~~~~~~~~~~

D. Gatton Sun Ray
Hybrid
Variable
Flower width 3–4 in. (8–10 cm)

This fine dendrobium, a cross between
Dendrobium dahlhousieanum v. *luteum*
and *D. Illustre*, was obtained in 1919
and registered then. It is a floriferous
hybrid with hundreds of flowers to a
mature plant.
Plate 93 (opposite)

Dendrobium

D. moschatum
The Himalayas to Burma, Thailand to
Laos
Spring
Flower width 1–2 in. (2.5–5 cm)

The genus name refers to the
epiphytic habit, meaning "living on
a tree." Some dendrobiums are
deciduous, but this one is an evergreen
and can grow to 6 ft. (1.8 m) high. The
blooms are musk-scented. This orchid
was introduced into cultivation about
1825 by Dr. Nathaniel Wallich.
Plate 94 (left)

D. nobile
South China, the Himalayas,
Thailand, Laos, Vietnam, Formosa
Spring
Flower width 3–4 in. (8–10 cm)

One of the deciduous dendrobiums,
this species was supposedly depicted
in Chinese drawings. The first live
plant in England was brought from
China by John Reeves, who purchased
it in the market at Macao about 1837.
The flowers form on upper nodes of
generally leafless cane pseudobulbs.
Many horticultural variants have been
produced (see plate 104).
Plate 95 (opposite)

152 Dendrobium

Dendrobium

D. phalaenopsis
Ceylon
Autumn
Flower width 3–4 in. (8–10 cm)

Originally found in northern Australia
and New Guinea, this singularly
beautiful orchid has arching stems of
many flowers. The color varies from
deep purple to pinkish white. It was
first described in the *Gardeners'*
Chronicle in 1880.
Plate 96 (opposite)

D. bigibbum v. *phalaenopsis*
Hybrid
Winter
Flower width 1 in. (2.5 cm)

A fine, flowering plant originally from
Australia, *D. bigibbum* takes the form of
the standard phalaenopsis. The variety
phalaenopsis has larger flowers than
the species, and its color varies from
white to purple.
Plate 97 (right)

Dendrobium

D. aggregatum v. majus
The Himalayas to Burma, India
Spring
Flower width 2 in. (5 cm)

This plant, small and compact, produces dozens of flowers on pendent scapes. Though a somewhat difficult variety to grow, it is an orchid of great charm and well worth the effort. Introduced by the Royal Horticultural Society of London, it bloomed for the first time in the collection of Mr. Warrison at Liverpool. The species name refers to the clustered pseudobulbs.
Plate 98 (right)

D. densiflorum
The Himalayas to Burma
Spring
Flower width 1–2 in. (2.5–5 cm)

Discovered by Dr. Nathaniel Wallich in the early nineteenth century, this species flowered for the first time in England in Messrs. Loddiges' nursery in 1830. The plant produces scapes from nodes along branches; the inflorescence resembles a large bunch of grapes with as many as thirty flowers per scape.
Plate 99 (far right)

Dendrobium

D. superbum
Hybrid
Autumn/winter
Flower width 5–6 in. (13–15 cm)

A deciduous orchid, this outstanding species was first discovered by Hugh Cuming in Manila about 1836 and it flowered in England in 1839, at Messrs. Loddiges' nursery in Hackney. The plant bears pendent leafless scapes, sometimes 4 ft. (1.2 m) long, with large scented blooms.
Plate 100 (far left)

D. Victoriae reginae 'Veronica'
Hybrid
Summer/autumn
Flower width 3 in. (8 cm)

Originally dedicated to Queen Victoria, the plant was described in the *Gardener's Chronicle* in 1897. It is an orchid of exceptional beauty, but due to its rarity it is seldom seen in collections today. It has been awarded the American Orchid Society's Highly Commended Certificate (HCC/AOS).
Plate 101 (left)

Dendrobium

D. superbum v. dearei
The Philippines
Autumn/winter
Flower width 5–6 in. (13–15 cm)

This orchid is the white form of
D. superbum. (See plate 100).
Plate 102 (left)

D. Christmas Chime 'Azuka'
Hybrid
Variable
Flower width 2–3 in. (5–8 cm)

D. Christmas Chime, one of the very
fine dendrobium crosses, is highly
recommended and always beautiful.
Introduced in 1974, it is a cross of
D. Ailing and D. Red Star. This cross
was awarded the American Orchid
Society's Award of Merit (AM/AOS).
Plate 103 (opposite top)

D. nobile 'Virginale'
Hybrid
Summer
Flower width 3–4 in. (8–10 cm)

This fine plant has large flowers that
last for many weeks. It is a highly
prized orchid.
Plate 104 (opposite bottom)

Lycaste

~~~~~~

L. aromatica 'Ivanhoe'
Mexico, Guatemala, Honduras
Spring
Flower width 2 in. (5 cm)

The genus is named after one of the
daughters of Priam, the last king of
Troy. The species *L. aromatica* was first
sent by Lord Napier from Mexico to
the Edinburgh Botanic Garden before
1826. 'Ivanhoe' is an improved form
and has received the Certificate of
Cultural Merit from the American
Orchid Society (CCM/AOS).
Plate 112 (opposite)

L. depeii
Mexico, Guatemala
Summer/autumn
Flower width 3–5 in. (8–13 cm)

Always a favorite, this orchid was first
described in 1830 as *Maxillaria depeii*.
The plant is easily grown and bears
many flowers. It grows to about 16 in.
(43 cm) tall, and the flowers, which
last for eight weeks, usually appear
before or when the new growth starts.
Plate 113 (above)

Lycaste

~~~~~~~~~~~~~~~~~~~~~~~~~~~~~~~~~

L. cruenta 'Linda'
Mexico, Guatemala, Costa Rica,
Ecuador
Spring
Flower width 2–3 in. (5–8 cm)

L. cruenta was discovered in Guatemala
by G. Ure Skinner around 1841. This
hybrid 'Linda' is an improved form
and won the American Orchid Society
Award of Merit (AM/AOS).
Plate 114 (left)

~~~~~~~~~~~~~~~~~~~~~~~~~~~~~~~~~

L. gigantea
Ecuador, Peru
Summer
Flower width 3–6 in. (8–15 cm)

As far as is known, this fine orchid first
bloomed in England in 1845, although
previous flowerings in Belgium may
have occurred. Once classed in the
genus *Maxillaria*, this species produces
flowers on erect stems. The flowers in
some ways resemble miniature
lampshades of the Tiffany type.
Plate 115 (opposite)

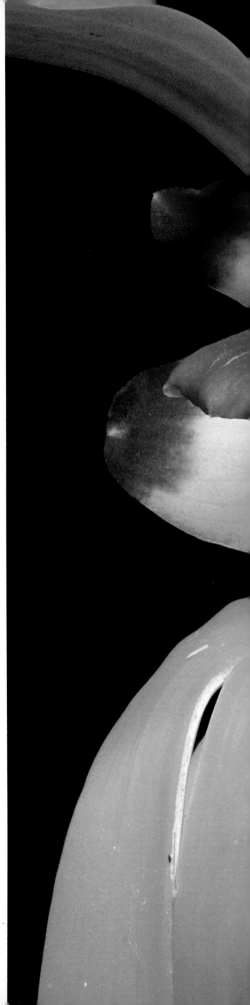

Lycaste

L. skinneri 'Fertility Gardens'
Guatemala
Spring/summer
Flower width 4–5 in. (10–13 cm)

The species, *L. skinneri*, is the national flower of Guatemala and an endangered species. The broad, papery-thin leaves are usually deciduous. 'Fertility Gardens' is an improved form, popular with hobbyists.
Plate 116 (left)

Maxillaria

M. grandiflora 'Puyo'
Peru, Ecuador
Summer
Flower width 4–5 in. (10–13 cm)

The typical species was collected by F. H. A. von Humboldt and Aimé J. A. Bonpland in 1816 and originally called *Dendrobium grandiflora*. Later, it was transferred to the genus *Broughtonia*, and then to *Lycaste*. Finally, in 1832 John Lindley placed it in the proper genus—*Maxillaria*.
Plate 117 (below left)

Pescatorea

P. dayana v. rhodacra
Colombia
Winter
Flower width 1–2 in. (2.5–5 cm)

This orchid with showy flowers was originally described by H. G. Reichenbach in 1874 in the *Gardener's Chronicle*. *Rhodacra* is one of the several color variations in this species.
Plate 118 (right)

Telipogon
~~~~~~~~~~~~~~~~~~~~~~~

T. tesselatus
Peru
Summer
Flower width 1–2 in. (2.5–5 cm)

From the cloud forests this rare, small
orchid is a treasure of color. Although
it is difficult to cultivate, this plant is
seen occasionally in choice collections.
Plate 119 (above)

Zygopetalum
~~~~~~~~~~~~~~~~~~~~~~~

Z. mackayi
Brazil
Winter
Flower width 3–4 in. (8–10 cm)

The typical form was introduced in
1826 by Mr. Mackay, of the Trinity
College Botanic Garden in Dublin. Its
strong perfume made it a British
favorite. A cloud forest dweller—living
at an elevation of 4,600 ft. (1400 m),
this orchid is often confused with *Z.
intermedium* but the flowers of *Z.
mackayi* are generally larger.
Plate 120 (opposite)

176   Zygopetalum

Zygopetalum

Z. 'John Banks'
Hybrid
Winter
Flower width 3–4 in. (8–10 cm)

This improved hybrid has more vivid
color than the typical species. A prized
plant with scented flowers, it is a cross
of *Z. blackii* and *Z. crinitum*.
Plate 121 (far left)

Z. intermedium
Brazil
Autumn
Flower width 2–3 in. (5–8 cm)

A species of singular beauty, it was first
discovered by Conrad Loddiges and is
sometimes classified as *Z. mackayi*,
which it resembles. It first bloomed in
1837 in the collection of Mr. Bowe of
Manchester. The plant grows to 24 in.
(61 cm) high.
Plate 122 (left)

178   Aeranthes

Aeranthes

~~~~~~~~~~~~~~~~~~~~~~~~~~~~~~~~~~~~~~

A. *arachnites*
Madagascar
Summer/autumn
Flower width 1–2 in. (2.5–5 cm)

The genus name refers to mist—or
air—flowers. The blooms are indeed
ethereal in appearance; the plant grows
up to 16 in. (41 cm) high. It was first
included in the genus *Angraecum* and
described as such in the *Botanical
Magazine*. This is an unusual and
lovely orchid.
Plate 123 (opposite)

Angraecum

~~~~~~~~~~~~~~~~~~~~~~~~~~~~~~~~~~~~~~

A. Ol Tukai 'Talisman Cove'
Hybrid
Winter
Flower width 3–4 in. (8–10 cm)

This is a recent hybrid between *A.
comorense* and *A. sesquipedale*. It blooms
around Christmastime with large,
impressive flowers.
Plate 124 (right)

Angraecum

A. *leonis* 'Jenny's Moonbeam'
Hybrid
Summer
Flower width 1 in. (2.5 cm)

Native to Madagascar, this showy
species was first described by H. G.
Reichenbach in 1885 as *Aeranthes leonis*.
J. Veitch put it into its proper genus in
1894. 'Jenny's Moonbeam,' an
improved cultivar, was awarded a prize
in the American Orchid Society's
Certificate of Cultural Merit (CCM).
Plate 125 (far left)

Ascocenda

Ascda. Cholburi
Hybrid
Summer
Flower width 3–4 in. (8–10 cm)

A handsome cross between *Ascocentrum*
and *Vanda*, this highly desirable plant
produces many flowers of almost
perfect shape.
Plate 126 (left)

Ascocentrum

A. *curvifolium*
The Himalayas
Spring
Flower width 1–2 in. (2.5–5 cm)

A dwarf orchid with bright cinnabar-
red flowers, it was at one time
classified both in the genera
Saccolabium and *Gastrochilus*.
Discovered by Dr. Nathaniel Wallich
in 1833 and called *Saccolabium
curvifolium* by Dr. John Lindley, it was
finally put in the proper genus by
Rudolph Schlecter in 1913.
Plate 127 (left)

A. *ampullaceum*
China to Malaysia
Spring
Flower width 1–2 in. (2.5–5 cm)

This handsome dwarf species has
bright flowers. Four of the nine known
species in the genus are in
contemporary collections, often
classified mistakenly under the genus
name *Saccolabium*. First described in
1832 by W. Roxburgh in *Flora Indica* as
Aerides ampullaceum, it was reclassified
to the genus *Ascocentrum* in 1913 by
Rudolph Schlecter.
Plate 128 (opposite)

Renanthera

~~~~~~

R. imschootiana
Burma
Summer
Flower width 2 in. (5 cm)

An epiphytic dwarf species, it is
distinguished by its dramatic flowers.
The plant is now on the endangered
species list.
Plate 142 (above)

Renanthopsis

~~~~~~

Rnthps. Shalimar
Hybrid
Summer/autumn
Flower width 2 in. (5 cm)

Hybridists have been crossing the
genera *Renanthera* with *Phalaenopsis* to
create other beautiful orchids.
Plate 143 (opposite)

Rhyncostylis (Saccolabium)
~~~~~~~~~~~~~~~~~~~~~~~~~~~~

R. gigantea
Burma, Thailand, Laos
Winter
Flower width ½–1 in. (1–2.5 cm)

This genus was founded by the Dutch botanist Karel Lodewijk Blume on the beautiful species commonly known as *Saccolabium blumei*. The genus name refers to the beaked column of the original species. A popular orchid with hobbyists, it has straplike leaves and pendent scapes of small scented flowers.
Plate 144 (opposite)

Rhyncostylis
~~~~~~~~~~~~~~~~~~~~~~~~~~~~

R. retusa
India, southeast Asia, the Philippines
Summer
Flower width ½–1 in. (1–2.5 cm)

The first notice of this species appeared in 1831 in *The Botanical Register* under the name *Sarcanthus guttatus*. Similar to others in the genus, the plant has straplike leaves and bears rather small pendent flowers, as many as 200 to a spike. It is commonly called the foxtail orchid and has an especially wide distribution.
Plate 145 (above)

Rhyncostylis

R. gigantea: **Sagarik's 'Orchidglade'**
Hybrid
Winter
Flower width ½–1 in. (1–2.5 cm)

A magnificent orchid with a sweet fragrance, it has brilliant flowers that are clustered on pendent scapes. The plum-red types of *R. gigantea* are rare in nature. Such select forms, however, can be obtained by seed methods of growing; Sagarik's 'Orchidglade' is a notable example. It holds the American Orchid Society's Award of Merit (AM/AOS).
Plate 146 (left)

Trichoglottis

T. philippensis v. *bracheata*
The Philippines
Summer/autumn
Flower width 3 in. (8 cm)

Although ranging from the Himalayas, throughout the Asiatic tropics to New Guinea, most plants of this genus are found in the Philippines. They have waxy, vibrantly colored flowers. Described by Dr. John Lindley in 1845, this plant is sometimes called *T. stauropsis.*
Plate 147 (opposite)

Vanda

~~~~~~

V. Rothschildiana
Hybrid
Autumn
Flower width 4–5 in. (10–13 cm)

This well-known orchid was one of the first blue vandas. It is a cross of *V. caerulea* and *V. sanderiana*. *V. sanderiana* was discovered by Messrs. Sander and Co. in 1882 and bloomed in England for the first time in 1883.
Plate 148 (above left)

V. Onomea
Hybrid
Summer
Flower width 3–4 in. (8–10 cm)

Because this desirable hybrid (above), with its flat-faced petals, has just blossomed, it displays a brilliant color.

On the facing page, the same orchid is shown, but its flowers have been open for many days and have started to fade. The color is dull, and the petals puckered. A cross of V. Rothschildiana and *V. sanderiana*, the orchid itself has been used extensively for hybridization.
Plates 149 (above right); 150 (opposite).

Vanda

~~~~~~~~~~~~~~~~~~~~~~~~~~~~~~~~

V. suavis
Java
Winter
Flower width 4–5 in. (10–13 cm)

Discovered by Thomas Lobb and introduced into England in 1846, this species has been used extensively for hybridizing. A large plant, up to 60 in. (1.5 m) tall, *V. suavis* is a star-burst-blooming climber. The flowers are stiff and fleshy, and the lip petal has an exceptionally intricate formation.
Plate 151 (left)

~~~~~~~~~~~~~~~~~~~~~~~~~~~~~~~~

V. Evening Glow
Hybrid
Summer
Flower width 4–5 in. (10–13 cm)

This winsome orchid, whose delicate coloring is a subtle mixture of pastel tints, blooms twice a year. It is a cross between V. Alice Fukunaga and V. Clara Shipman Fisher.
Plate 152 (opposite)

Vanda

V. cristata
Nepal, Bhutan
Summer
Flower width 2–3 in. (5–8 cm)

This orchid was first gathered in 1818
by Dr. Nathaniel Wallich at high
elevations in Nepal, and it bloomed at
the Royal Botanical Gardens at Kew
sometime later.
Plate 153 (left)

Polystachya

P. albescens
Africa
Summer/autumn
Flower width ½ in. (1 cm)

The genus name is from the Greek
polys meaning many and *stachys*
meaning ear grain, and refers to the
resemblance of the flower to a grain
plant. This unusual orchid has
miniature flowers.
Plate 154 (opposite)

Ansellia

A. africana v. nilotica
Tropical and South Africa
Summer
Flower width 3–4 in. (8–10 cm)

The typical species is closely allied to
Ansellia gigantea. Known as the leopard
orchid, *A. africana* was described in
1847 by H. G. Reichenbach. The
variety *nilotica* was first collected in
1860 and has brown markings, deeper
and richer than in the standard species.
Plate 155

Catasetum

~~~~~~

C. pileatum (*bungerothii*)
Venezuela, Colombia, Ecuador
Autumn
Flower width 4–5 in. (10–13 cm)

This orchid of unusual beauty has a
unique flower form and an intense
fragrance. It is Venezuela's favorite
flower. It was introduced in 1882 by
H. G. Reichenbach in the *Gardener's
Chronicle*.
Plate 156 (opposite)

~~~~~~

C. Orchidglade 'York'
Hybrid
Spring
Flower width 4–5 in. (10–13 cm)

This typical variety is a well-known
cross between *C. pileatum* and *C.
expansum*. Bred in 1974, "York" is an
improved form, and was awarded the
American Orchid Society's Highly
Commended Certificate (HCC/AOS).
Plate 157 (above right)

~~~~~~

C. Francis Nelson
Hybrid
Summer
Flower width 3–4 in. (8–10 cm)

This hybrid produced by two Brazilian
species (*C. trulla* × *C. fimbriatum*)
bears exquisite flowers of maroon and
green.
Plate 158 (below right)

Catasetum

C. 'Fanfair'
Hybrid
Summer/autumn
Flower width 3–4 in. (8–10 cm)

This catasetum variety is known for its unusual flowers. The genus name comes from the Greek *kata*, down, and the latin *seta*, referring to the two appendages at the base of the column in flowers. This is a dwarf orchid.
Plate 159

Cymbidium

_C_. Jill Katalinka
Hybrid
Winter
Flower width 3–4 in. (8–10 cm)

A fine hybrid with waxy flowers, this
very floriferous cymbidium stays in
bloom for several weeks.
Plate 160

Cymbidium

C. Ivy Fung 'Demke'
Hybrid
Winter
Flower width 2–3 in. (5–8 cm)

One of the dwarf cymbidiums with desirable maroon flowers, many clustered on a pendent scape.
Plate 161 (left)

C. Red Imp 'Red Tower'
Hybrid
Winter/spring
Flower width 4 in. (10 cm)

This is a cross between C. Alderman and *C. pumilum* produced in 1963. The typical species, *C. pumilum* has been used as a parent for many cymbidium hybrids.
Plate 162 (below left)

C. Tapestry 'Red Glory'
Hybrid
Winter
Flower width 5–6 in. (13–15 cm)

Large flowers with dramatic markings characterize this fine orchid. It is a cross between C. Khyber Pass and C. Voodoo.
Plate 163 (opposite)

Cymbidium

C. devonianum
India
Winter
Flower width 3–4 in. (8–10 cm)

This orchid was introduced to England about 1837, finally flowering there in 1843. It remained a rare plant until 1865. The species is variable in color and is one of the few species cymbidiums still cultivated.
Plate 164

Cymbidium

C. Orchid Conference
Hybrid
Winter
Flower width 3 in. (8 cm)

This highly distinctive product of man's orchid-breeding ingenuity truly lives up to its name. A luxuriant row of tightly clustered flowers adorns the gracefully arching scape. Orchid Conference is a cross between C. Sola and *C. pumilum*.
Plate 165

Cymbidium

C. **Alexette**
Hybrid
Winter
Flower width 3–4 in. (8–10 cm)

The dainty refinement of this
exquisite orchid is a perfect
counterpart of its name. It is a cross
between C. Alexanderi and C. Janette.
Plate 166 (opposite)

C. **Joan of Arc 'White Velvet'**
Hybrid
Winter
Flower width 3–4 in. (8–10 cm)

The name says it all: This excellent
cultivar is known for its perfect flower
shape and color. It was awarded the
American Orchid Society's Award of
Merit (AM/AOS).
Plate 167 (above right)

C. **Nona 'Goldilocks'**
Hybrid
Winter
Flower width 3–4 in. (8–10 cm)

This is one of the fine yellow hybrids
of great substance and color.
Plate 168 (below right)

Cymbidium

C. Peter Pan 'Greensleeves'
Hybrid
Winter
Flower width 2–3 in. (5–8 cm)

A famous miniature or dwarf plant, this
early flowering cross between *C.
ensifolium* and C. Miretta bears dozens
of flowers on a stalk. The plants are
floriferous and flowers last for weeks.
Plate 169

Cycnoches

C. ventricosum v. *chlorochilum*
Panama, Colombia, Venezuela
Spring
Flower width 3–4 in. (8–10 cm)

Because of the shape of the flower, this species (center) is popularly known as the swan orchid. It was discovered by Karl Moritz in Venezuela in 1838 and was sent to the Berlin Museum. The orchid flowered in England for the first time about the same year. The red orchid (top) is a *Dendrobium phalaenopsis* hybrid. The orange orchid (bottom) is a *Laelia cinnabarina*. The marked differences among orchids are made apparent by comparing the three included here. Note the lip of the cycnoches; usually the species grows with the lip at the bottom of the flower—the reverse is the case here. Plate 170

Galeandra

G. devoniana
Colombia, British Guiana
Summer
Flower width 3 in. (8–10 cm)

This very handsome species has grassy leaves and grows to about 50 in. (1.3 m) tall. First described by M. R. Schomburg about 1838, it was sent to Dr. John Lindley. The species is named after the Duke of Devonshire, who was then a successful cultivator of orchids. *G. devoniana* can be grown as a terrestrial or as an epiphyte.
Plate 171 (left)

Grammatophyllum

G. speciosum
Malaysia
Summer
Flower width 2–3 in. (5–8 cm)

Discovered about 1825 in Java, the treelike plant can grow to an enormous size. It was misnamed several times in the next 25 years but finally bloomed in Messrs. Hackney's nursery in 1852. Its brown color is not often seen in orchids, but in this genus there are hundreds of these lovely flowers on each plant.
Plate 172 (opposite)

Miltonia

M. Goodhope Bay 'Raindrops'
Hybrid
Summer
Flower width 2–3 in. (5–8 cm)

A special cultivar between M. Lilac
Time and M. Woodlands made in
1976, this is a prolific bloomer and has
outstanding color as well as long-
lasting flowers.
Plate 182 (left)

M. Evergreen Joy 'Carmen Cole'
Hybrid
Summer
Flower width 3–4 in. (8–10 cm)

This famous pink orchid, which has
enjoyed great popularity, is an
outstanding cross between M.
Etendard and M. Edmonds, created in
1979.
Plate 183 (below left)

M. Dearest
Hybrid
Variable
Flower width 3–4 in. (8–10 cm)

Commonly called either pansy orchid
or ballerina orchid, this lovely hybrid
has dramatic flowers borne on pendent
scapes. It is a cross between M.
Dolores Hart and M. Champagne.
Plate 184 (opposite)

Miltonia

M. spectabilis v. moreliana
Rio de Janeiro, southern Brazil
Summer
Flower width 3–4 in. (8–10 cm)

M. spectabilis is the species on which the genus was founded. The variety *moreliana* (darker in color) was first sent to Charles Morel of Saint-Monde, near Paris, in 1846. The plant grows to 20 in. (.5 m) high and has grassy foliage.
Plate 185 (far left)

M. regnalii
Brazil
Autumn
Flower width 3–4 in. (8–10 cm)

This unusually large-flowered *Miltonia* was discovered by Dr. Regnell in 1846 although it was not seen again until 1855 in an exhibition at Hamburg.
Plate 186 (above left)

M. Crimson Crest × *Odonticidium carryphyllum*
Hybrid
Summer
Flower width 3–4 in. (8–10 cm)

This plant is a fine example of man improving on nature.
Plate 187 (below left)

Oncidium

O. ampliatum v. *majus*
Central America
Spring
Flower width ½–1 in. (1–2.5 cm)

Discovered about 1831 and gathered by
G. Ure Skinner and Jósef Warscewicz
in Central America, it grows in partial
shade and produces tall, wandlike
stems covered with bright yellow
blooms. It is called the turtle orchid
because of the shape of the
pseudobulbs.
Plate 200 (opposite)

O. macranthum
Ecuador, Columbia, Peru
Summer
Flower width 1–2 in (2.5–5 cm)

The earliest evidence of this species
was a single flower in the herbarium of
the Spanish botanists Hipólito Ruiz
Lopez and José Antonio Pavon. It was
probably introduced about 1780; the
locality given was Guayaquil, in
Ecuador.
Plate 201 (above)

Oncidium

O. Makaii 'Gotah'
Hybrid
Summer
Flower width 2–3 in. (5–8 cm)

This oncidium brings bright yellow
and brown colors to the orchid world.
It was awarded the American Orchid
Society's Award of Merit (AM/AOS).
Plate 202 (above)

O. Wilbur 'Elizabeth'
Hybrid
Summer
Flower width 1–2 in. (2.5–5 cm)

Naturally small but beautiful, this
prize-winning orchid (AM/HOS) bears
exquisite racemes of flowers. It is a
cross between O. Catherine Wilson
and O. Caledonia in 1979.
Plate 203 (right)

Oncidium

~~~~~~~~~~~~~~~~~~~~~~~~~~~~~~~~

O. splendidum
Guatemala, Honduras
Spring
Flower width 3–4 in. (8–10 cm)

A popular orchid with cactuslike
leaves, and long scapes bearing many
flowers, it was first discovered in 1852
in Guatemala but not generally grown
until 1862.
Plate 204

Oncidium

O. Boissense
Hybrid
Autumn/winter
Flower width 2–3 in. (5–8 cm)

This fine orchid, a cross between *O. forbesii* and *O. varicosum*, dates back to 1924. Both parents are native to Brazil.
Plate 205 (opposite)

Wilsonara

W. Five Oaks Golden Leaf
Hybrid
Variable
Flower width 2 in. (5 cm)

Oncidium tigrinum is a prime parent of this cross. The yellow and brown coloring, indicative of the genera, show through with dramatic effect. It was awarded the American Orchid Society's Award of Merit (AM/AOS).
Plate 206 (right)

Trichopilia

T. tortilis v. alba
Mexico, Guatemala
Spring
Flower width 5–6 in. (13–15 cm)

The genus of *Trichopilia* was founded on this orchid. Not usually grown, this overlooked orchid from a rain forest habitat was first described by Dr. John Lindley in 1836. It is a showy, fragrant species and it bloomed for the first time in England in 1839.
Plate 207 (left)

T. suavis
Costa Rica, Columbia, Panama
Summer
Flower width 7 in. (18 cm)

This orchid was supposedly first discovered in 1848 by Jósef Warscewicz in Costa Rica in the cordillera at an elevation of 5,000 to 8,000 ft. (1,500 to 2,400 m). It bloomed for the first time in England in 1851. The plant has clustered pseudobulbs, leaves up to 12 in. (31 cm) long, and bears large flowers that hug the rim of the pot.
Plate 208 (opposite)

Societies and Periodicals

Membership in any society listed below brings with it the society's valuable publication.

The American Orchid Society
The American Orchid Society
  Bulletin
6000 South Olive Street
West Palm Beach, FL 33405
$28/yr., published monthly

Australian Orchid Review
P.O. Box 60
Sydney Mail Exchange,
  Australia 2012
published quarterly

Cymbidium Society of America
The Orchid Advocate
5902 Via Raal
Carpinteria, CA 93013
$12.40/yr., published bimonthly

The Orchid Digest Corporation
The Orchid Digest
c/o Mrs. Norman H. Atkinson
P.O. Box 916
Carmichael, CA 95609-0916
$18/yr., published bimonthly

The Orchid Review
5 Orchid Avenue, Kingsteignton
  Newton Abbot,
Devon TQ12 3HG England
published monthly

South African Orchid Journal
c/o Hugh Rogers, editor
10 Somers Road
Clarendon
Pietermaritzburg 3201,
  South Africa
published quarterly

South Florida Orchid Society
The Florida Orchidist
13300 SW 111th Avenue
Miami, FL 33176
$12/yr., published quarterly

Bibliography

Ames, Blanche. *Drawings of Florida Orchids*. 2d ed. (*Explanatory Notes by Oakes Ames*). Cambridge, Mass.: Botanical Museum of Harvard University, 1959.

Ames, Blanche, and Donovan S. Correll. *Orchids of Guatemala*. Chicago: Field Museum of Natural History, 1952–53. (Fieldiana: Botany, Vol. 26, Nos. 1 and 2.) Two volume supplement by Correll, 1966.

Bailey, Liberty Hyde. *Standard Cyclopedia of Horticulture*. 3 vols. New York: Macmillan, 1935.

Blowers, John W. *Pictorial Orchid Growing*. Maidstone, Kent, England: John W. Glowers, 1966.

Boyle, Frederick. *The Culture of Greenhouse Orchids: Old System and New*. London: 1902.

Boyle, Louis M. *Growing* Cymbidium *Orchids and Other Flowers*. Ojai, Calif.: El Rancho Rinconada, 1953.

Cady, Leo, and T. Rotherham. *Australian Orchids in Color*. Sydney: Reed, 1970.

Chittenden, Fred J. *Dictionary of Gardening*. 4 vols. Oxford: Clarendon Press, 1951.

Correll, Donovan S. *Native Orchids of North America, North of Mexico*. New York: Ronald, 1950.

Cox, J. M. *Cultural Table of Orchidaceous Plants*. Sydney: Shepherd, 1946.

Craighead, Frank S. *Orchids and Other Air Plants of the Everglades National Park*. Coral Gables, Fla.: University of Miami Press, 1963.

Curtis, Charles H. *Orchids: Their Description and Cultivation*. London: Putnam, 1950.

Darwin, Charles. *The Various Contrivances by Which Orchids Are Fertilized by Insects*. New York: Appleton, 1892; London: Murray, 1904.

Davis, Reg. S., and Mona Lisa Steiner. *Philippine Orchids*. New York: William Frederick Press, 1952.

Dodson, Calaway H., and Robert J. Gillespie. *The History of the Orchids*. Nashville, Tenn.: Mid-America Orchid Congress, 1967.

Dunsterville, G.C.K. *Introduction to the World of Orchids*. Garden City, N.Y.: Doubleday, 1964.

Fennell, T.A., Jr. *Orchids for Home and Garden*. New York: Rinehart, 1956; rev. ed., 1959.

Garrard, Jeanne. *Growing Orchids for Pleasure*. South Brunswick, N.J.: Barnes, 1966.

Ghose, B. N. *Beautiful Indian Orchids*. Darjeeling: Ghose, 1959; 2d ed., 1969.

Gilbert, P.A. *Orchids: Their Culture and Classification*. Sydney: Shepherd, 1951.

Graf, Alfred Byrd. *Exotica 3: Pictorial Cyclopedia of Exotic Plants*.

Rutherford, N.J.: Roehrs, 1963.

Grubb, Roy, and Ann Grubb. *Selected Orchidaceous Plants*. Parts 1–3. Caterham, Surrey: Roy and Ann Grubb, 1961–63.

Hawkes, Alex D. *Encyclopedia of Cultivated Orchids*. London: Faber and Faber, 1965.

———. *Orchids: Their Botany and Culture*. New York: Harper & Row, 1961.

Hogg, Bruce. *Orchids: Their Culture*. Melbourne and Sydney: Cassell, 1957.

Hooker, Sir Joseph Dalton. *A Century of Orchidaceous Plants*. London: Reeve & Benham, 1851.

Kramer, Jack. *Growing Orchids at Your Windows*. New York: Van Nostrand, 1963.

———. *Growing Hybrid Orchids*. New York: Universe, 1983.

Kupper, Walter, and Walter Linsenmaier. *Orchidees*. Zurich: Service d'Images Silva, c. 1955; *Orchids*. Edinburgh: Nelson, 1961.

Lecoufle, Marcel, and Henry Rose. *Orchids*. London: Crosby, Lockwood, 1957.

Logan, Harry B., and Lloyd C. Cooper. *Orchids Are Easy to Grow*. Chicago: Ziff-Davis, 1949.

Moulen, Fred. *Orchids in Australia*. Sydney: Australia Edita, 1958.

Noble, Mary. *You Can Grow* Cattleya *Orchids*. Jacksonville, Fla.: Mary Noble, 1968.

O'Brien, James. *Orchids*. Edinburgh: T. C. and E. C. Jack, 16 Henrietta Street. 19TK.

Oca, Rafael Montes De. *Hummingbirds and Orchids of Mexico*. Mexico: Fournier, 1963.

Osorio, Luis F. *Orquideas Colombianas*. Medellin: Bedout, 1941. Text in Spanish and English.

Richter, Walter. *Die Schonsten aber sind Orchideen*. Radebeul: Neumann, 1958. Translated and revised as *The Orchid World*. New York: Dutton, 1965.

Rittershausen, P.R.C. *Successful Orchid Culture*. London: Collingridge: New York: Transatlantic Arts, 1953.

Sander, David. *Orchids and Their Cultivation*. rev. ed. London: Blandford, 1962.

Sander, Fred. *Reichenbachia: Orchids Illustrated and Described*. 4 vols. London, 1888–93.

Sander & Sons. *Complete List of Orchid Hybrids*. St. Albans, Herts.: Sander, 1946. Addenda, 3 vols., 1946–48, 1949–51, 1952–54.

———. *One-Table List of Orchid Hybrids, 1946–60*. 2 vols. St. Albans, Herts: Sander, 1961. Addenda, 1963, 1966.

———. *Sander's Orchid Guide*. rev. ed. St. Albans, Herts.: Sanders, 1927.

Sander's List of Orchid Hybrids. London: Royal Horticultural Society. Addenda, 1961–70, 1971–75, 1976–80.

Schelpe, E.A.C.L.E. *An Introduction to the South African Orchids*. London: Macdonald, 1966.

Schweinfurth, Charles. *Orchids of Peru*. 4 vols. Chicago: Field Museum of Natural History, 1958–61. (Fieldiana: Botany, Vol. 30, Nos. 1–4.)

Summerhayes, V. S. *Wild Orchids of Britain*. London: Collins, 1951.

Thomale, Hans. *Die Orchideen*. Ludwigsburg: Ulmer, 1954.

Veitch, James & Sons. *A Manual of Orchidaceous Plants*. 2 vols. London: James Veitch and Sons, 1887–94. Reprint. Amsterdam: Ashler, 1963.

Watkins, John V. *ABC of Orchid Growing*. 3d ed. Englewood Cliffs, N.J.: Prentice-Hall, 1956.

Watson, William and H. J. Chapman. *Orchids: Their Culture and Management*. rev. ed. London: Gill, 1903.

White, E. A. *American Orchid Culture*. rev. ed. New York: De La Mare, 1942.

Williams, John G., and Andrew E. Williams. *Field Guide to Orchids of North America*. New York: Universe Books, 1983. Illustrated by Norman Arlott.

Williams, Louis O. *The Orchidaceae of Mexico*. Tegucigalpa, Honduras: Escuela Agricola Panamericana, 1952.

Withner, Carl L. *The Orchids: A Scientific Survey*. New York: Ronald, 1959.

Wright, N. Pelham. *Orguideas de mexico*. Mexico: La Prensa Medica Mexicana, 1958. Bilingual text.

Acknowledgments

Grateful acknowledgment is made to the following institutions for permitting use of reproductions in their holdings:
Academy of Science, Botanical Library, San Francisco, California; American Orchid Society, Inc., 6000 South Olive Street, West Palm Beach, Florida; Art Institute of Chicago, Chicago, Illinois; Bancroft Library, University of California, Berkeley, California; East Asiatic Library, University of California, Berkeley, California; Freer Art Gallery, Washington, D.C.; Hunt Botanical Library, Pittsburgh, Pennsylvania; Massachusetts Horticultural Society, Boston, Massachusetts; Metropolitan Museum of Art, New York, New York; Museum of Fine Arts, Boston, Massachusetts; Royal Botanic Gardens at Kew, Richmond Surrey, England.

My personal thanks go to the following individuals who gave freely of their time and knowledge:
Hermann Pigors of Oak Hill Gardens, Dundee, Illinois; Eugene Hausermann of Hausermann Orchids, Villa Park, Illinois; Steven Christofferson of The Garden District, Yountville, California; Margaret Ilgenfritz; Warren Kelly of Orchid World, Int., Miami, Florida; Beall Orchids, Vashon Island, Washington; Robert Jones; R. Desmond of the Library of the Royal Botanic Gardens at Kew, Richmond Surrey, England; Paul C. Hutchison of Escondido, California; George Lawrence, formerly of the Hunt Botanical Library, Pittsburgh, Pennsylvania; Anton Christ of the University of California Botanic Gardens (Orchid Division), Berkeley, California; Henry Teuscher of the Montreal Botanic Gardens; Gordon W. L. Dillon and Merele Reinnika, former officers of the American Orchid Society, Inc., West Palm Beach, Florida; and a special note of deep appreciation to my editor, Susan Costello of Abbeville Press, New York.

Many of the photographers who worked with me on this project went far beyond the call of duty to capture on film the plants I wanted represented. Joyce R. Wilson shot and reshot orchids almost on a weekly basis for many months. Guy Burgess of Colorado provided a select group of fine orchids. Hermann Pigors of Oak Hill Gardens and Charles Marden Fitch of New York contributed many excellent slides from their files. Andrew R. Addkison of Jackson, Mississippi, kept a record on film of the orchids in my collection; some of his best shots are included. To all these people (and many more I probably have forgotten) my deepest thanks for their interest, enthusiasm, and patience.

Index

Page numbers in italics refer to illustrations

Photo Credits

Illustration Credits